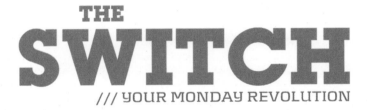

THE SWITCH
/// YOUR MONDAY REVOLUTION

Doug Spada

Published by CrossSection
940 Calle Negocio #175
San Clemente, CA 92673
800-946-5983
crosssection.com

Book + Jacket design by Crosssection

Set in Museo & Rockwell with special guest font Kontrapunkt

Printed in the USA

ISBN 978-0-9899537-3-3 (paperback)
ISBN 978-0-9899537-4-0 (Kindle)

T . G . I . M .

Thank God It's Monday

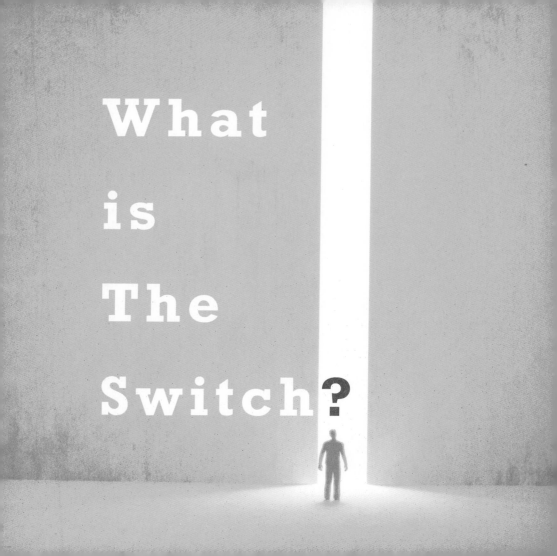

THE PRACTICE OF KEEPING GOD SWITCHED ⏻N EACH MONDAY!

IT'S ABOUT WORKING WITH GOD, NOT FOR HIM OR WITHOUT HIM. IT'S ABOUT MAKING HIS PRESENCE A PRIORITY AT WORK.

FINDING GOD'S POWER ON MONDAY!

IT'S A CHANGE, A TURN-AROUND; IT'S A MONDAY REVOLUTION!

CONTENTS:

What's Inside:

Step 1: *Monday Morning Moan* ————— *14*

Step 2: *The Switch* ————— *38*

Step 3: *Wired for Work* ————— *64*

Step 4: *Short Circuit* ————— *94*

Step 5: *CROSSwired* ————— *118*

Step 6: *Mpowered* ————— *144*

Appendices:

A: *About our Research* ————— *169*

B: *About the Author* ————— *170*

C: *Acknowledgments* ————— *172*

D: *Eternal Job Security* ————— *173*

E: *WorkLife.org Resources* ————— *174*

A NOTE FROM THE AUTHOR

Do you look forward to Mondays? Yea, I know, Mondays and work sneak up on the best of us. Research shows that Mondays bring a whole lot of trouble. Did you know that more heart attacks occur on Monday morning than any other day of the week? Add panic attacks, stress and discouragement to the mix and you have more than most of us ever want to deal with.

I know this well. Many years ago, I experienced a personal crisis. God had little involvement in my work life and as a result I let my work and character collapse. My success was superficial, my spiritual life was in shambles, and I watched my family slip through my fingers. God restored my family, but I had to look at work and life in a completely different way.

As followers of Christ, we all need a Monday revolution. After all, knowing Christ personally has given you a new life. But how does it show up at work on Monday? God's power and grace will change your work on Monday! If you let it. This is the purpose of The Switch, to let God empower your work.

It does not matter who you are or what you do. Whether you are an executive in your company, a medical first responder, a mom diapering babies or a technician, Mondays are about to change for you. When you switch on this one day your entire work week will change.

The Switch is a six step series that will take you on an experiential journey unlike most. It will be fun and surprising, yet challenging. We have created some user friendly tools to help you keep God top of mind and Switched ON each Monday. You will learn to work WITH God instead of working WITHOUT Him.

And get this; it only takes 6 committed Mondays to SWITCH ON your entire life at work!

This is why we developed The Switch. I don't want you to suffer as I did from working with God Switched OFF. (You can find my full story in the book Monday Morning Atheist).

I genuinely desire for you to find God's power, His purpose, His plan for your work on Monday. Believe me, you will soon be saying "Thank God it's Monday (TGIM)!"

Come on, let's make The Switch!

Doug

Doug Spada
WorkLife Founder & CEO

WHAT'S INSIDE THE BOOK

The Switch six step series is designed to guide you through a dynamic progression over six sessions that ends with finding a renewed perspective and God's power for Mondays and your work.

As you move through each step, here's what you'll find inside each step of The Switch.

1. **OVERVIEW:** This is a short concise teaching that will give you a good understanding of each step's principles and highlights.

2. **MONDAY CHECK-IN:** A quick time to meet with others and track your progress. You will get to plug into the Monday Moan Meter. What's your moan time?

3. **SHOWTIME:** Hold on for this fast moving feature video to spur on your thoughts and discussions.

4. **WORKING IT OUT:** Time to go a little deeper. Tackle these interactive questions with personal reflection. Some serious - some fun!

5. **SWITCH IT ON:** Let's go do it now. Practice makes perfect. Monday to-do's and a quick wrap up for the session.

Step 1	Step 2	Step 3
Monday Moan	The Switch	Wired for Work

A FEW HELPFUL TIPS...

- Flying solo is okay, but it's best if you nab a friend, co-worker, or a small group to experience The Switch six step series together.

- Expect change. Get comfortable with experiencing authentic change and spiritual growth. You're going to love it.

- There are no expected answers or performance—only new Mondays!

- Warning: This is a life altering experience. It's not "just another study to make your way through".

- The Overview in each step is critical. And the videos really rock! So don't skip these.

- Practice-Practice-Practice! The Monday Must Do's, Moan Meter and Text Alerts make The Switch stick.

- Cheer each other on. Celebrate each person's path towards their own Monday revolution.

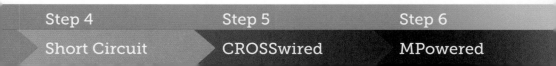

Step 4	Step 5	Step 6
Short Circuit	CROSSwired	MPowered

MONDAY MORNING MOAN

Welcome to the start of your Monday Revolution.

We use the word "revolution" because it is powerful, meaning: "turn around" or "a fundamental change." Your work and your Mondays are about to change for the better. Mondays may be the new Friday for you.

This journey will transform how you experience Mondays, your least favorite day of the week, in a life-altering way. Instead of moaning, can you imagine Mondays that are filled with more joy, more purpose, more life! Thank God it's Monday!

OVERVIEW

In our work culture, we often think of the week as an uphill climb toward Wednesday—which we lovingly refer to as "Hump Day." Wednesday is not only the day during which we get over that hump, but it's also when we're finally able to see the weekend not too far off. The whole journey of the week, it seems, is to get to Friday. The frequency of the saying, "Thank God It's Friday," is evidence of that.

By Friday evening you are already engaged in the different activities, chores, and tasks of the weekend: dinner obligations, household repairs, soccer games, social events and more.

Then Sunday rolls around—only one day left before Monday. Maybe you go to church, grab some lunch, try to relax, and then squeeze in some quality time with your spouse, family, or friends (and don't forget to fix the thing you blew off on Saturday). Whoa, you need a nap already! But here comes Monday—Sunday is a slight pause before Monday is right in your face again!

The reality is that even by Sunday evening most people are already sliding into a Monday morning moan.

Makes a great ending to the weekend, huh?

Monday is a day unlike any other because it launches our entire spiritual work week!

Okay, here we are at Monday morning. How are you feeling? Before you answer that, let's shift gears for just a minute.

When it comes to living out your faith in practice, have you noticed that it's hard to maintain your spiritual edge on Monday? Where is the God who was so clearly with you on Sunday? On Sunday it seems easy to be with God. But Monday is a whole different story. The rules change. It's a new world—we hustle and work to put out fires.

Interestingly, God also works on Mondays. The Bible says God is a worker—that you are His workmanship. Your work matters to God. He is with you and invites you to join Him in what He is doing in your life—especially at work.

You spend more hours working than in any other activity in life. Why waste it? Work is also where you face most of your faith challenges while in full view of the majority of your relationships.

What if God actually cares more about your Monday than Sunday?

Your work is valuable to God. He never intended any part of your life to be kept apart from a relationship with Him. In fact, God has big plans for your work—plans to bless you and to bring him glory.

Clearly God wants more for you than just surviving Mondays and drifting through a spiritually neutral workweek. He created you to Thrive! He wants to give you the mind of Christ as you work so you can experience His presence. He also desires to give you His power so you can Thrive. He wants to transform your Monday moaning into Monday thriving.

It comes down to this: You will be making The Switch to a revolutionary new view of your working life. You're starting a Monday Revolution! *A Change.* With this revolution should come the realization that you have a purpose in life and a purpose in work. You can absolutely have a more energetic and meaningful life during your workweek and at home. But, the alternative to finding and claiming your purpose is defaulting back into your Monday moans.

Monday is the gateway to your entire spiritual work week. When you start your week poorly, you may find you are unable to recover for several days or even weeks. On Mondays you need to focus on thriving not surviving. If you do, you will start to see the new things God is doing in and through your work. Meditate on this promise God gives you as you move through this six step experience.

See, I am doing a new thing! Now it springs up; do you not perceive it?
I am making a way in the wilderness and streams in the wasteland.
—Isaiah 43:19 (NIV)

Without God filling our life at work, it's no wonder why work, and especially Mondays, feel like such an empty experience; and why work so often causes real pain for us in life. Often, we think about switching God off in dramatic situations. In reality, many of us end up drifting from God at work in ways that are far more subtle.

The demands of life constantly pull against what God wants for us, drawing us away inch by inch. In fact, even things that seem good according to the world can be subtle ways to separate us from what is truly good according to God.

Those gradual and seemingly small steps eventually place us much farther away than we ever realized. For many of us, this slow steady drifting away from God has happened in our work. It can be a drift caused by a series of choices and habits that may seem mostly harmless at the time but have a way of breeding consequences in our lives over time.

That's why it may be hard for us to admit or even realize that God simply no longer seems relevant to us in the way we work. We have conditioned ourselves to work without God. We work like we are on our own, like it's all depending on us. We have switched God off at work, choosing to go ahead blindly.

(pg 26 Monday Morning Atheist, the book)

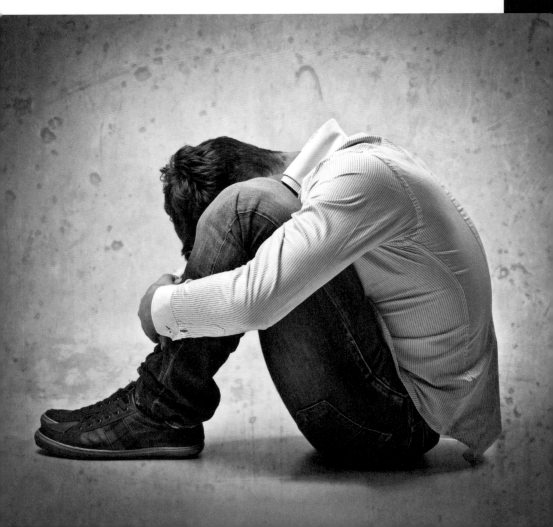

The fact is, Monday is a day created by God for you to Thrive! You are created by God to live and work in a way that is more abundant and more fulfilling. In fact, each Monday opens the door to an entire week of God possibilities—abundance—and comfort in knowing Mondays serve a purpose in God's plan. Just listen to what Jesus himself said about your life (even on Mondays) in John 10:10.

> *I came to give life with joy & abundance."*
>
> —*John 10:10 (The Voice)*

In other words, you can thrive, flourish, prosper, succeed, bloom, blossom, increase, and grow well. Your Mondays should be new and purposeful each week, regardless of your weaknesses or circumstances. You know, only God can deliver results like that. He does and he will for you—right sized just where you are. Regardless of where your Mondays are now, there is so much more for you!

This single day of Monday can change your entire workweek for the better. Surrender your Mondays to God and you will experience your own Monday revolution! ⏻

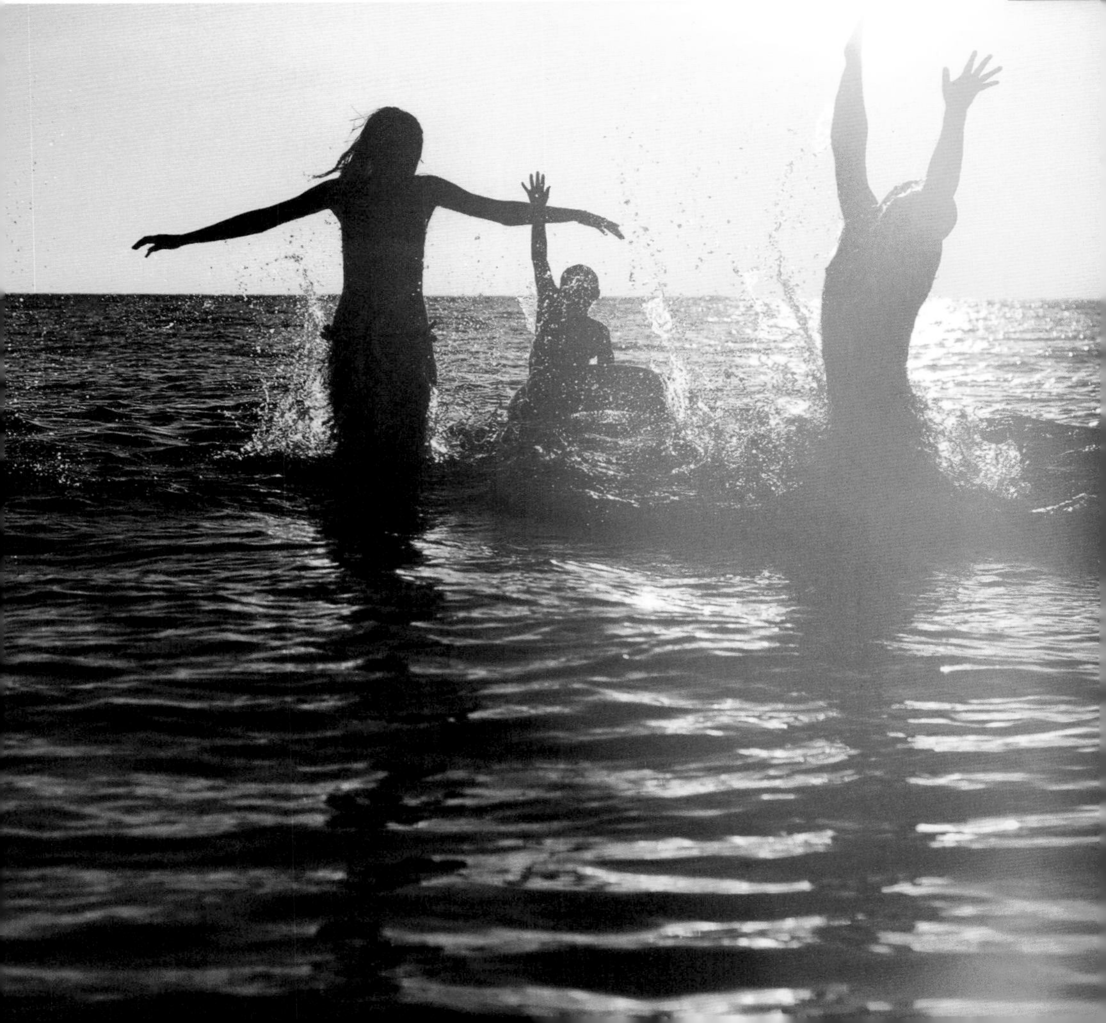

SHOWTIME (FEATURE VIDEO)

This week in Showtime we will be looking at some serious moaning. Start the video, sit back, and hold your moan.

Try It: Take 5 seconds as a group and give us your best Monday morning moan. Go ahead and get it out!

Share This: How long do you moan or complain on Monday Mornings? What do you moan about?

How did that moan feel? You're at the start of The Switch and soon you won't be complaining or moaning on Mondays anymore.

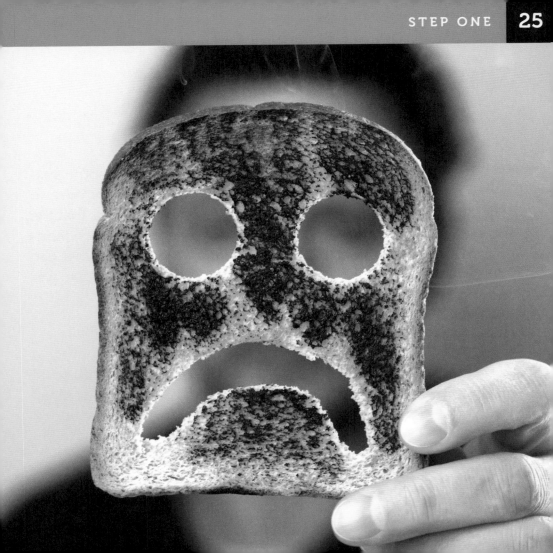

MONDAY MOAN METER (CHECK IN)

MY MONDAY MOAN
(SOMEONE READ THIS TO GROUP)

A lot of times just thinking about Monday mornings gives us some anxiety—almost a sense of dread. That anxiety is something you have to deal with 52 times a year, every year. Informal research shows that the average person spends about 10 minutes or more moaning each Monday morning, turning Mondays into more of a "Moan-Day". What can we do about all of this whining, complaining, and griping on Mondays?

INTRODUCING THE "MONDAY MOAN METER"
Each of us is going to track our Moan Time each Monday.

Let's try it now: Think about your past Monday, how would you score yourself on the Monday Moan Meter to the right? Circle your Moan Time now. Remember a moan can be an attitude or an internal outlook.

Discuss: Share your Moan Time and what may be causing it with the group.

MOAN: *def. verb* - to grumble, whine, complain, groan, or gripe either in thought or word.

WORKING IT OUT (GOING DEEPER)

Many of us can see a reflection of ourselves in the feature video. What about you? The truth is, each of us is a card-carrying member of the "Moan-Day Club" in one way or another.

....

TAKE THIS CHALLENGE TO FIND OUT.

How does this Monday attitude and outlook affect our thoughts, behaviors, and relationships?

1. In 30 seconds, jot down 4 words that describe Mondays. Go.

    a. _____

    b. _____

    c. _____

    d. _____

Share how these words affect your expectations of each Monday. Do they affect your behavior as well as those around you?

_____

_____

_____

2. Have a group member read this verse out loud:

...because God is always at work in you to make you willing and able to obey his own purpose. Do everything without complaining or arguing. Philippians 2:13–14 (GNT)

Q: Why do you think we complain, moan, and grumble so much about work?

_____

_____

_____

3. Someone read this out loud **with passion**:

Let's get real! Do we really want to live a week to week cycle that starts with Moan-Day and ends with a pathetic TGIF outlook of the workweek? Really? For 52 weeks a year, every year for the rest of our lives? This would be 70% of life—5 out of 7 days looking forward to just 2 days off and then starting all over.

Let's not rob ourselves, and God, by living anything less than an attitude of TGIM: Thank God Its Monday! And then watch what happens!

Q: What would it take for you to honestly say "Thank God it's Monday" and really mean it?

- How would your attitude have to change?

- What would your weekend look like?

- Your Monday mornings?

- Your thoughts? Your actions?

Your Challenge: Can you commit the next 6 Mondays to an all-out focus on keeping God switched ON?

I'm changing my Thank God it's Friday to Thank God it's Monday. #mondayswitch

SWITCH IT ON (PRACTICAL STEPS)

Okay okay, we know you're just as excited as this guy to get working. Each week, we'll throw some Monday Must Do's at you. (By the way, we're impressed you're being so adventurous.)

....

MY MONDAY MUST-DOS:

(Go to MondaySwitch.com/STEP1)

☐ **EVERYONE: SIGN-UP** for the **"MONDAY TEXT ALERTS"**!
(ONLY on Mondays and ONLY for the next 6 weeks) Go to:
MondaySwitch.com/Step1 and follow the simple step.

☐ **FOLD** an Origami Moan Meter. Go to MondaySwitch.com/Step1 and
download. For one week keep it in a visible place.

☐ Next Monday: **DECLARE** at least 7 times out loud "Thank God it's Monday."
We're changing attitude here. You've got to say it to believe it.

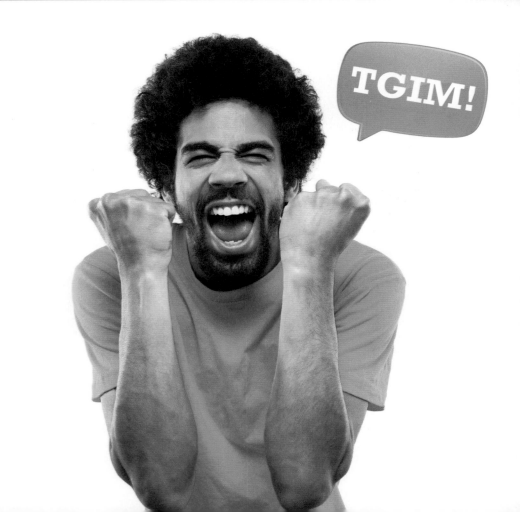

"The Monday Text Alerts were just what I needed. They arrived for 6 Mondays and helped me stay ON at work!" —*Angela*

"Loved the texts I got on Monday! They were inspiring and sometimes quite funny." —*Bob*

Keep God Switched ON this Monday!

Get this simple and fun tool that really helps. FREE

SIGN UP NOW for "MONDAY TEXT ALERTS"!

(ONLY on Mondays and ONLY for 6 weeks)

Go to MondaySwitch.com/Step1 and follow the simple steps.

Visit this QR code to sign up.

MY MONDAY JOURNEY LOG

Journey log starter questions:

1. What is one thing you see improving most on Monday?

    (Ex. your attitudes, decisions, relationships, peace or purpose)

    _____

2. What specifically would you like to see God do this next Monday?

    _____

    _____

3. Who can you pray for at work this week?

    _____

    _____

MY PRAYERS & NOTES

THE
SWITCH

It's Time to Flip The Switch!

You're one step into your Monday Morning switch. How did it go last week? Most likely it wasn't perfect, but that's to be expected. This is a process, a mind and heart shift that doesn't just happen overnight. We spend years building habits, and now we are changing them for the better.

Change will involve more than just tracking your Monday Moan Time each week. So, Step TWO will help expose The Switch. The Switch is actually the purposeful or unconscious act of switching God ON or OFF while working. Your Mondays are about to change!

OVERVIEW

You do many involuntary things in your life just by habit. You can drive your car without consciously thinking about turning the steering wheel in a certain direction. Do you think about riding a bike or just pick it up and ride? You can try brushing your teeth with the opposite hand to see how well a habit has formed. Most habits are automatic in our lives. Most habits serve us well, or at the very least don't cause many problems.

However, you also have involuntary things in your life that you would not consider good. You can probably think of a few of those, right? What about being habitually late or blaming someone else when you aren't able to fully complete a job. Maybe little white lies to a co-worker. Maybe taking home a few supplies from the office. If you are like most people, you also have a general tendency to involuntarily switch God OFF when working. Most of us struggle with this as much as moaning and complaining.

Most of us have never consciously thought about this habit of Switching God OFF. It takes both awareness and intentionality to keep God switched ON in your work. However, paying attention to that switch promises a breathtaking payoff. Once you notice and respond to welcoming God into your work you find that your work and life begins to Thrive in spite of circumstances or challenges. Lean in. Focus. Keeping God Switched ON at work, especially on Monday, is a wise thing to do!

THE SWITCH:
It's the practice
of keeping God
switched ON
each Monday

Monday mornings are prime time for trouble as we have seen! Moaning and complaining is a major indicator that your Monday Switch is already OFF! But what is behind all this moaning and complaining? We need to look a little closer to find out.

FACT: Our view of Mondays and work has a much deeper meaning. The Monday Morning Moan along with the attitudes and behaviors we exhibit are contaminated by a serious underlying and often hidden flaw. We have left God out of our work, and in doing so, we've not only shut out His presence but also His power in our work lives on Monday.

Moaning and complaining are serious issues, but switching God OFF on Monday breeds even more trouble, and it can be very difficult to recognize this struggle. Let's briefly examine some of the ways it plays out in our lives.

We have left God out of our work, and in doing so, we've shut out not only His presence but His power in our work.

The actual work and character issues facing us today are numerous. As we try to navigate work without God, our souls suffer many bumps and bruises. We often feel like a slave to our schedule as we battle with stress and discouragement. Our spouse may be consumed by his or her career, or maybe we're the one being consumed. There are conflicts surrounding office politics such as gossip, slander, favoritism, and criticism. Some of us have significant discontent with our paycheck or position. We struggle with anger and the pressure to fudge our ethics, and sometimes we come face-to-face with sexual temptation at work.

A big issue today is worry over job insecurity; this is now a way of life for many. But even when the economy is rolling happily along, it never really delivers what it promises. The intoxicating effects of money only mask the underlying pain and great costs our work imposes on the rest of our life. Many of us are addicted to our work. It has consumed us. We are never off. We are always on. Our wayward way of working has cost our mar-

riages and family relationships dearly. Carrying the unending stress of it all has even undermined our health. The rampant illnesses of heart disease, obesity, hypertension, diabetes, and depression are in many cases symptoms of the unbalanced way we have learned to work.

(pg 28-29 Monday Morning Atheist, the book)

Does any of this resonate with you? You can see what we are talking about—huh? Worse yet, both the root and the seriousness of these issues are aggressively fed by the involuntary state of working without God on Monday—The Switch.

When God is involuntarily or intentionally switched OFF we don't address the serious flaw in our independent nature and we suffer the consequences. Morals easily fluctuate with an 'everything is relative' mindset. Expediency can become an end all, with right and wrong becoming more blurred by the press of the work week. How easily we loose our integrity and wholeness!

Here's the hard truth. Switching God OFF is actually a form of practical atheism. You heard it right—atheism. We all know the general definition of an atheist—someone who does not believe in God. Most

of you reading this would adamantly deny you're an atheist! That is good! But, what do our actions, our behaviors really say about who we are and who we follow on Mondays?

Atheist

def. Someone who doesn't believe in God.

Monday Morning Atheist

def. Someone who believes in God but who works like He does not exist.

So, we see our feelings about Mondays go much deeper than just a moan—it's actually God's people practicing atheism on Monday morning. A Monday Morning Atheist is defined as someone who believes in God but who works like He does not exist.

Unfortunately, this describes most of the working body of Christ on Monday mornings across the world. What about you? Can you relate to this? Does your moan and your Monday struggle have deeper roots? You must see it—be aware of it—before you can continue to make The Switch in your work life.

> *Even though most of us who are reading this book probably believe in God, at certain times in our work lives we function just like atheists. None of us are entirely exempt—we all do it on occasion. It's just a question of when and in what area we turn God OFF while working. Whether The Switch has always been off, or is just mostly off, the truth is the same –for many of us, we often work as if God does not exist. When we approach our work week without including God, we have to be honest: we are practicing Monday Morning Atheism.*
>
> (page 27 Monday Morning Atheist, the book)

Can you honestly believe in God yet practice Monday Morning Atheism at the same time? Absolutely! Most do it all the time. The crucial

question is can you follow God and bring honor to His reputation while working?

Without God's presence and power at work you will experience difficulty and have trouble dealing with the issues of any given week. You may stumble, get disoriented, and sometimes hurt yourself, your co-workers, or even your family. You may have moved in a direction that seemed right, but ended up in the wrong place or in a bad situation.

Who would want to work this way? Living a Moan-day to TGIF Friday attitude for 52 weeks a year can be miserable. God's presence and power will enable you to better experience all of the good that God has planned for you. Remember, He wants you to increasingly Thrive. The answer is simple, but not always easy. Switching God ON in your work requires a different way of thinking and acting. It requires a choice to be different—to form new habits.

"The worst lies are not the ones we tell, but the ones we live."

There is a spiritual switch happening every Monday—the Monday Switch! Actually, millions of Christians are working with their switch OFF most, if not all of the time. But, that is now changing. You are part

of a Monday Revolution that right now is expanding around the world. A complete change in the way we see Monday!

Please remember, you are not alone! You are part of something new that God is doing through His people! Stay committed! Do it for yourself! Do it for your family and community! But most of all, do it for your God! Stay Switched ON!

> *But if serving the Lord seems undesirable to you, then choose for yourselves this day whom you will serve, whether the gods your ancestors served beyond the Euphrates, or the gods of the Amorites, in whose land you are living. But as for me and my household, we will serve the LORD.* Joshua 24:15 (NIV)

Eventually, serving the Lord in and through your work will become a more natural part of your life. Remember how you automatically handle the steering wheel of your car? In the same way, new habits will be forming throughout our time together.

As a believer in Jesus Christ you have been given the Holy Spirit who lives in you, empowering you to flow in God's strength and ability. You will soon be able to say, "Thank you, God, that I am no longer practicing Monday Morning Atheism!" And that will bring a smile to God's face!

Remember, THE SWITCH is the purposeful or unconscious act of switching God ON or OFF while working. Stay purposefully switched ON this Monday! You can do it. Mondays are changing for you.

MONDAY MOAN METER (CHECK IN)

HERE WE GO TEAM. HOW DID YOU WORK THIS PAST MONDAY?

Mark your Moan Time now.
Circle your Moan Time on the Monday Moan Meter to the right.

Discuss with Others:
What was the cause of any Moan Time this past Monday?

....

MY MONDAY CHECK IN:

done?

 I SIGNED UP for the "Monday Text Alerts".
    If you haven't, visit www.MondayText.com now.

☐ **I READ** STEP TWO Overview

☐ **I DECLARED** "Thank God it's Monday" 7 times last Monday

☐ **I FOLDED** my Origami Moan Meter and put it in a visible place.

MOAN: *def. verb* - to grumble, whine, complain, groan, or gripe either in thought or word.

SHOWTIME (FEATURE VIDEO)

This week in Showtime we take a peek behind our Monday moans to see what's really going on. Start the video and let's explore.

Consider: Wow, did you hear those people talk about Monday and work? One even said Monday sucked!

Share: Everyone share one feeling or situation that you identified with from the workers who shared in the video.

No one is exempt from Monday Morning Atheism. Your Monday Moans are just a symptom of a deeper spiritual issue.

"The Worst Lies are not the ones we tell, but the ones we live." #MondaySwitch

WORKING IT OUT (GOING DEEPER)

Things just got a little more serious, didn't they? Monday Moaning is only a symptom of some deeper spiritual issues.

FACT: All of us switch God OFF sometimes.

....

MONDAY MORNING ATHEIST **DEF.:**
Someone who believes in God but who ***works like He does not exist.***

Q: Based on this definition, do you frequently practice Monday Morning Atheism? **YES | NO** (each person share with group)

Q: If you had to guess, what percent of your work week do you believe is Switched OFF? In other words, working like God does not exist—ignoring Him. (share this with each other)

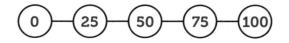

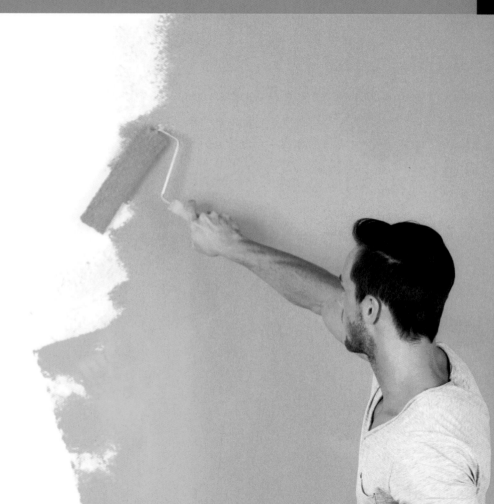

READ

Someone read this Scripture to the group:

> *Whoever looks intently into the perfect law that gives freedom and continues in it—not forgetting what they have heard, but doing it—they will be blessed in what they do.* —James 1: 22-25 (NIV)

DISCUSS

"not forgetting…, but doing it" Pretty strong words for us.

SHARE a recent situation or challenge at work that could have had a better outcome if God was Switched ON.

_____

_____

_____

_____

_____

TRY THIS

Identify one work project, decision, or relationship in which you could more fully Switch God ON in thought or action this coming Monday.

(Each person share one situation)

SOMEONE READ THIS OUT LOUD:

"The worst lies are not the ones we tell, but the ones we live."

SHARE/DISCUSS AS A GROUP: Think about your life at work. Where is this statement most true? What can you do about it?

PRAY TOGETHER

There is somebody in your group that is facing a situation or decision at work right now. Do something now! Pray for them in a special way.

(maybe do this each time you meet as a group)

SWITCH IT ON (PRACTICAL STEPS)

This guy needs to calm down! Are you ready to take on next Monday? Keep in mind: we are what we DO, not just what we think.

....

MY MONDAY MUST-DOS:

(Go to MondaySwitch.com/STEP2)

- [ ] **THE SWITCH QUIZ:** Go to MondaySwitch.com/Step2 and take a short 5 minute Switch Quiz. Why? To help identify your personal spiritual Switch Challenges.

- [ ] **DOWNLOAD** a digital Switch graphic background at MondaySwitch.com/Step2 Keep it on your phone / computer for one week.

- [ ] **My MONDAY JOURNEY LOG:** spend a few minutes before next session and log what God is doing on your Mondays.

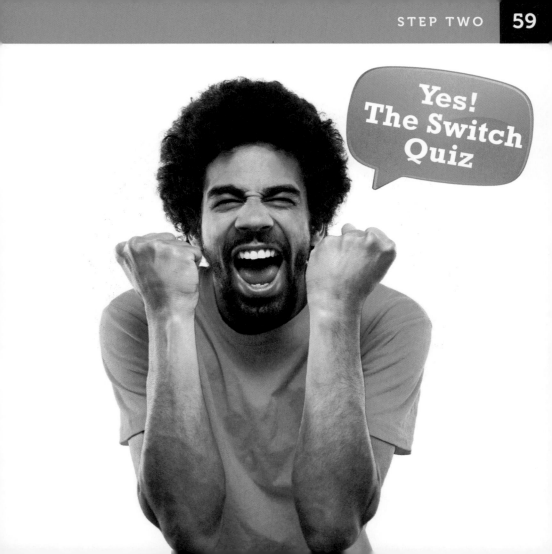

Yes!
The Switch
Quiz

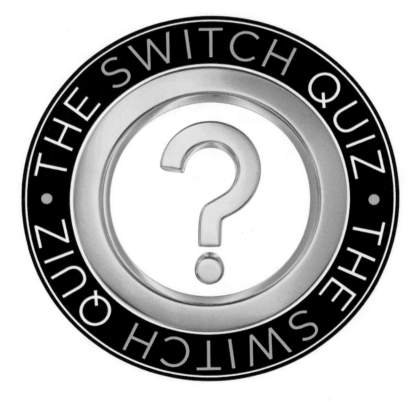

www.SwitchQuiz.com

TAKE THE SWITCH QUIZ NOW

Just 5 Minutes! This tool is based on 8 years of research and will help you find your most challenging work issues. You will get a FREE report via email and also see comparison results from other workers worldwide.

FILL IN FROM YOUR SWITCH QUIZ REPORT:

#1 switch challenge_____

#2 switch challenge_____

#3 switch challenge_____

MY MONDAY JOURNEY LOG

Journey log starter questions:

1. What is one thing you see most improving on Monday?
    (Ex. your attitudes, decisions, relationships, peace or purpose)

    _____

2. What specifically would you like to see God do this next Monday?

    _____

    _____

3. Who can you pray for at work this week? Did you?

    _____

    _____

MY PRAYERS & NOTES

WIRED
TO
WORK

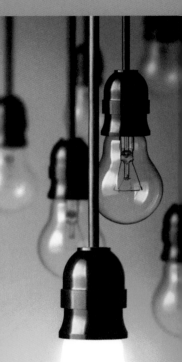

Wired to Worship God on Monday!

Welcome to Step Three of The Switch. Last session, we learned about the practice of Monday Morning Atheism. Not pretty sometimes, huh? Let's move away from that now!

In this session, we will uncover a core belief that is essential to thriving at work. Switching God ON requires an understanding of God's view of work.

The big idea in this session is "Work is GOOD". Your Mondays are going to be different: more joy, and more purpose, less moaning. Let's find out why God says work is GOOD.

OVERVIEW

Growing up I was warned by my parents to watch out for "bad" 4-letter words. For some reason they would pop into my head just trying not to think about them. One has likely popped into your mind already; a bad word that evokes negative emotions. Unfortunately, the word "WORK" often conjures a similar negative emotion. **But is work really just another 4-letter word?**

Many of us have questions about work that never get answered, like, "Why do I work?" and "Who created work?" Whether you enjoy work or not, ignoring the answers to these questions will certainly lead to the practice of Monday Morning Atheism. What if work is not what you think it is?

Questioning the point of our jobs is a gut-check no one can avoid, "Why work?" This question inevitably stops all of us in our tracks, and it is not satisfied by simple answers. It is, in fact, a question to us from God. We can try to ignore it. We can feed it temporary fixes. We can bribe ourselves with our paycheck. We can even be distracted momentarily from the problem with the false hope of greener pastures. Yet, under the surface, it remains unresolved and keeps bubbling back up within us. Why Work?

The questions are unavoidable: Why in the world am I doing this? Does what I do count for something? Is it worth all the trouble? What is the point of my work? What difference will it really make in the end? We spend most of our waking hours working, but the purpose and meaning of the actual work we do often eludes us.

(pg 85-86 Monday Morning Atheist, the book)

So, is work really just another 4-letter word? Well, yes, but not in the way you are programmed to think. In fact, God has another 4-letter word for work, "Good." Genesis tells us that on the sixth day, after God finished the greatest construction project ever—the work of creation—He looked back on all of His work and said "It is GOOD." Did you know on the very day He had created animals, birds, fish, man, and woman, He also created something else?

Did you know God actually created work? He produced a workplace called Eden for Adam and Eve, a place for them to work. It was a vital part of the plan and helped define their purpose on earth. Surprising, isn't it? Know-

Not only is work itself good, but it is actually a form of worship.

ing that work is "good" and that it was created by God is an eye-opener for most people. Work is described by culture in many ways—including "a necessary evil." You don't hear many people standing around talking about how great work is—yet, God Himself says it is GOOD.

> *God's view of work is so important that He headlined it in the very first chapter of the Bible. God originally created work to be experienced in the context of a moment by moment intimate relationship with Him. From the very beginning, the Bible paints a picture of man's spiritual bond with God in the Garden of Eden as a working relationship.*
>
> (pg 87 Monday Morning Atheist, the book)

The first glimpse God gives us of Himself in scripture is a picture of Him working—and working hard. He spent each day working to shape and create a perfect world— the heavens, earth, water, land, plants, trees, animals and human beings.

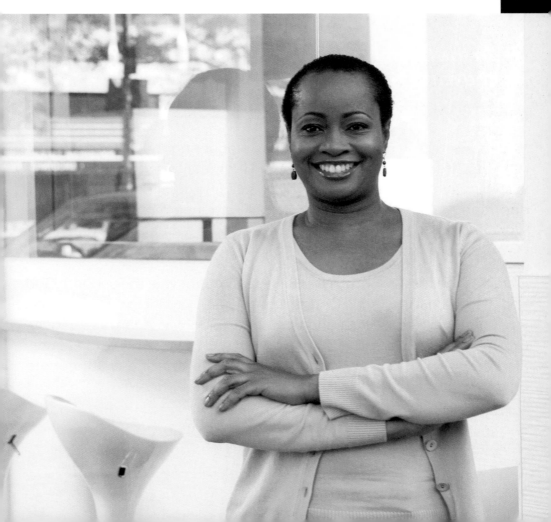

In the beginning God created the heavens and the earth." Genesis 1:1 (NIV)

What God did in those six days was staggering, but He didn't stop working after that. He continues working until this very moment. He is still creating, sustaining, providing, blessing, healing, loving, giving, answering, rescuing, delivering, forgiving, redeeming and more. His work is, quite literally, never done. Your God is a creator, a worker, and He says work is GOOD.

God was the first to work in the Bible, and Adam was the second. God had created him to work. God not only models work for man, He defined man's first job. I guess you could say God was Adam's employer. God had a purpose and a job for Adam and Eve even before He created them. Their job was to tend (work) God's amazing creation here on earth—to rule over the land and the animals.

The Lord God placed man in the Garden of Eden to tend and watch over it. Genesis 2:15 (NLT)

Not in a single place does the Bible say Adam and Even didn't want the job or dreaded going to work each day—nowhere. Since their job was part of their work in paradise, it is safe to assume that work provided a source of joy. And, just like everything else God created for them, it provided a way to enjoy close relationship with the Lord himself.

God delights in what we do. Like Adam, He designed us uniquely and He enjoys our work like a father delights in a child. If a human father feels delight in the work of his children, no matter how simple, then imagine how much more God, the perfect Father, delights in our work. While we may often feel that our work is unimportant, He delights in our efforts as a reflection of His glory in creation. "Whatever you do, do it all for the glory of God" (1 Corinthians 10:31, NIV)
(pg 109 Monday Morning Atheist, the book)

Here is the key point: When God created man it was not in the same manner as when He created the earth, the moon, stars, or other wild animals. Man was created in God's image. Therefore, we are image-bearers of God at work. Not only were you made differently, you were designed with a unique purpose in mind. In all of creation, it was man alone who was made to be in relationship. Animals, birds

and even the fish in the sea are able to breath, communicate and re-produce—but only man is able to develop a friendship with the Lord himself. You were created to honor God with every aspect of your life, especially work. We were created as workers in the beginning, and Christ redeemed us as workers.

Take a minute and think about this: Jesus lived on this earth for 33 years. Most of His adult life was spent working in his dad's woodshop. We can only imagine the amazing products He produced! Jesus, the Son of God, Savior of the world, labored as a common worker for most of his adult life. This is perplexing unless our heavenly Father was teaching us this critical lesson: work is GOOD and it reflects His character.

So, why did Jesus work? Because he saw what His father did—not only His earthly father, Joseph, but more importantly He watched His heavenly Father work. Jesus always did what His Father did, as He stated in John 5:19 (NASB) "Truly, truly, I say to you, the Son can do nothing of Himself, unless it is something He sees the Father doing; for whatever the Father does, these things the Son also does in like manner."

Man was created in God's image. Therefore, we are image-bearers of God himself at work.

Did you catch that?—"in like manner"—Jesus worked in like manner. As followers of Christ, we are called to imitate Jesus—to be like Jesus—to work in like manner. We should be working just like Jesus worked, with joy, with purpose, and without Monday Morning Moans.

> *Follow my example, as I follow the example of Christ.* *Corinthians 11:1 (NIV)*

So, God wired you to work in like manner. This makes sense since we are created in His image. Therefore, the way God works, the way Jesus worked, has everything to do with the way you should work. FACT: This is impossible with your Switch OFF, when you are blinded in any way by Monday Morning Atheism.

Let's switch gears and clear up another common misunderstanding that's sure to change some thinking. Have you ever heard of work being referred to as "cursed"? Have you ever viewed your work as less than holy or not equal to other religious activities? This is simply not true—and it causes most Christians to immediately switch off at work.

The truth many never see is that work was created by God before disobedience (what the Bible calls sin) entered the world—it was while Adam and Eve still lived in paradise when God presented Adam with the idea and purpose of his job on earth. It was part of what God considered "GOOD" and was part of the perfect world in which Adam and Eve lived before sin entered the picture.

What if work is not what you think it is and neither is God?

What happened between the sixth day of the creation and present day to change the way we feel about work so drastically? Simple: A bunch of distortion. Adam and Eve disobeyed God and started a cycle of sin that you and I fight to this day. One of the many outcomes of this is the way in which we tend to view work. Originally, it was an expression of joy and love with the Creator, but then we began to compensate by either idolizing work or rejecting work. Despite the sweat and struggle added to man's work from sin, it did not stop being good. It just started being a bit harder. Work is still GOOD because it comes from the very

character of who God is and His purpose for you; it is still His creation and it is still GOOD.

So, without any added duty or performance, your work (no matter what it is) has "God value." No forced religious duty or spiritual act adds anything more to how God views your work; it has eternal purpose by itself. Your work has built-in value. Period. Working your best and honoring God makes Him rejoice over you. God smiles when he watches you work well.

There is yet another thing that stands in our way. Many of us struggle to see God as a dad who really cares about us and our work. Sure, we think He loves us, because that's His job, right? But do we believe He really likes us? We think of God as being far away—not interested in our work—kind of cold. We overlay our distant view of God onto our struggles at work, which ends up playing in our heads like this: "Well, work is actually punishment from God and we just have to put up with it." Hence, your Monday Moan.

Can anyone find joy and purpose in their work with a belief or feeling like this? We usually don't—so we just switch God OFF. Our view of God himself distorts our attitude about work—often making it a dread. Sure, work is hard at times. Some love it and some hate it. No matter what

your personal situation is, it does not change the truth. Work is GOOD. Our God, our Heavenly Father, is not distant and He does not check out when you boot up your computer or punch the clock at work.

Not only is work itself GOOD, but it is actually a form of worship. Avodah (Ah'-voe-dah) is a Hebrew word used in the Bible that has two different, yet intertwined meanings: work and worship. Our work is truly a form of worship to God himself! Whether you are a plumber, an executive, a parent, a nurse, a salesperson—whatever you may do— you have the privilege to stay switched ON and worship your God with your entire life. Mondays are changing for you now. ⏻

Whatever you do, work at it with all your heart, as working for the Lord, not for human masters, since you know that you will receive an inheritance from the Lord as a reward. It is the Lord Christ you are serving. Colossians 3:23-24 (NIV)

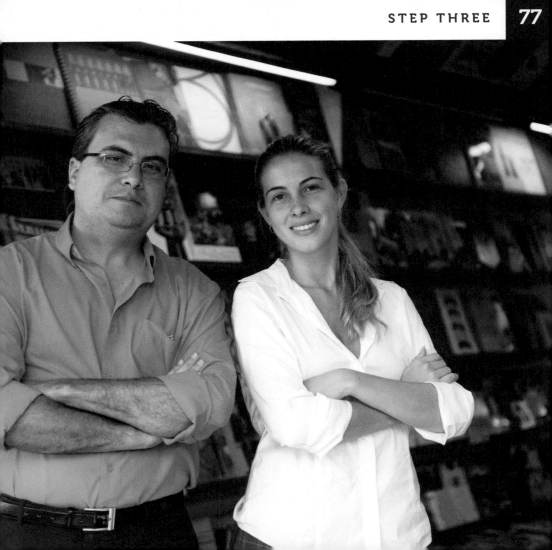

MONDAY MOAN METER (CHECK IN)

WORK IS GOOD SO WHY THE MOAN?
HOW DID LAST MONDAY GO?

Mark your Moan Time now.
Circle your Moan Time on the Monday Moan Meter to the right.

Discuss with Others:
It is pretty easy to feel that moan—huh?
What was the cause of any Moan Time this past Monday?

....

MY MONDAY CHECK IN:

done?

☐ **I COMPLETED THE SWITCH QUIZ** and wrote down my Switch Challenges
in last session. If not, go to www.SwitchQuiz.com now.

☐ **I READ STEP THREE** Overview

☐ **I DOWNLOADED** a Switch graphic for my mobile device or desktop

☐ **MONDAY JOURNEY LOG** - I logged my God experience.

MOAN: *def. verb* - to grumble, whine, complain, groan, or gripe either in thought or word.

SHOWTIME (FEATURE VIDEO)

Let's get Showtime started. Your view of work will not stay the same after this. Start the video and let's GO. The big idea for this step is "Work is GOOD".

Be Honest: Raise your hand if you think your work is GOOD? Go ahead! How many are holding your hands up?

Share: Share in your group why it is so hard to feel like work is GOOD and that God is right there WITH you.

You are made in God's image.

A worker just like He is.

God calls your work "GOOD".

"God says my work is Good!"
#MondaySwitch

WORKING IT OUT (GOING DEEPER)

Your work has "God value". In fact, God created work so that you could experience the Father's joy and love as you work. Although work did become harder after sin entered the world, it is still "GOOD" because **God is good**, and work is a part of God's character.

....

ANSWER THIS:
Which would you rather have:

1. LESS work to do, or

2. MORE work you actually enjoy doing?

Go around room and choose 1 or 2. Why did you answer this way? Discuss.

_____

_____

_____

GOD AS FATHER AT WORK

In the video we saw how God is present at work and walks with us. He is a loving Father that cares about all the details. We are image bearers of God at work.

Q: How can knowing, seeing, and sensing God WITH you right there at work change your work day?

Your Attitudes?_____

Your Decisions? _____

Your Relationships?_____

"WORK IS GOOD" ACTION STEP

God says work is GOOD and asks you to work like Jesus.
Last week you took The Switch Quiz. Now let's put it to work.

List Your #1 Switch Challenge (see page 61):

_____

_____

YOUR ACTION STEP FOR THIS WEEK:

Focusing on your #1 Switch Challenge this coming week—Identify two
practical things you will do this week to improve it. List them below.

A: _____

B: _____

Do these steps & share with group next week

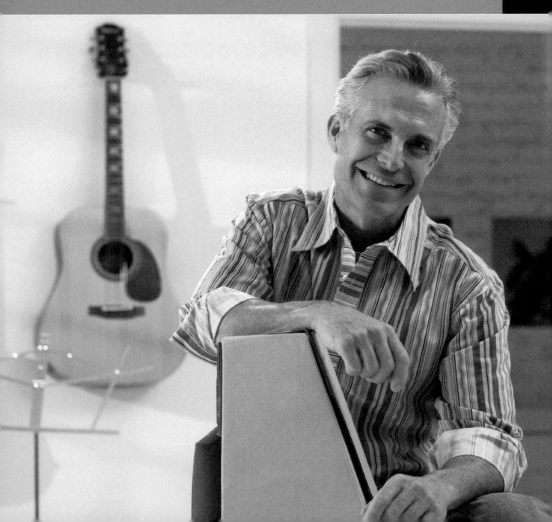

"WORK IS GOOD" 10 COMMANDMENTS

Go to the end of this Step and find the "10 Commandments". Some-one volunteer to start by reading the 1st Commandment out loud. Each person read one commandment.

Question for each of you:

Q: Which one of these 10 Commandments would most help you with your personal **#1 Switch Challenge**?

Choose One (1-10?)_____

(Discuss with group)

_____

_____

READ AND SHARE

Whatever you do, work at it with all your heart, **as working for the Lord, not for human masters...** Colossians 3: 23-24 (NIV)

Share: What does it practically look like for you to work with God in-stead of an organization or person?

TAKE A MINUTE

Someone pray for the entire group.
Pray that we could see our work as God sees it.

SWITCH IT ON (PRACTICAL STEPS)

God wired him to work that way. I would be excited too!
Let's start this next Monday morning with God switched ON.

....

MY MONDAY MUST-DOS:

(Go to MondaySwitch.com/STEP3)

 "WORK IS GOOD" Action Step (see page 84)
Be sure to TAKE this action & report back to the group next week.

 SHOUT OUT "WORK IS GOOD" 7 TIMES ON YOUR DRIVE TO WORK.
Doing this might even cut your moaning and complaining down a bit this
week. Remember, the Moan Meter tells all!

 "WORK IS GOOD" 10 Commandments
Go to MondaySwitch.com/Step3 and send to at least three of your friends
on facebook or twitter. Mention #MondaySwitch in your post

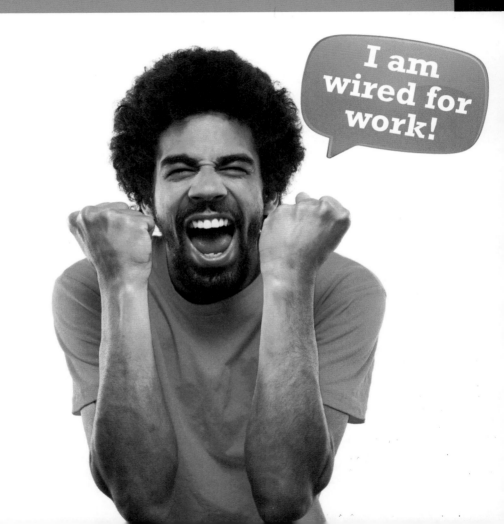

"WORK IS GOOD" 10 COMMANDMENTS

Download poster and share at MondaySwitch.com/Step3
(Forward to 3 Friends and post in your workspace)

1. **Trust in God only** (Proverbs 3:5-6)
   Trust in no one but God. People will disappoint you but God will not. His love is absolute. His plans for you are for your good.

2. **Worship God only** (Exodus 20:5)
   Who or what do you serve? Don't make your job, your company, or your boss a god. Put your God first in life and your work.

3. **Use God's name respectfully** (Matthew 15:17-19)
   Don't swear! It hurts God's heart and makes it difficult for your co-workers to see your faith in Jesus.

4. **Take one day a week to rest** (Genesis 2:2)
   God worked 6 days during creation and then took one day to rest. Do the same. This shows trust in God and helps you work well and avoid burnout.

5. **Respect and obey your boss.** (Ephesians 6:5-8)
   You need to respect and obey your boss because you don't know what it's like to be in his or her shoes. Besides, you ultimately work for God.

6. **Protect and respect human life** (2 Thessalonians 3:1-2)
   Emotional, mental, spiritual, and physical manipulation, abuse, and violence are not part of God's plan. Don't do it at work or anywhere else.

7. **Be true to your spouse** (Matthew 19:8-9)
   Attention and affection from others are very common and tempting. Honor your wedding vows. Crossing the line is wrong and destructive.

8. **Don't take what belongs to others** (2 Corinthians 7:1-2)
   Stealing can take many forms; materials, money, and productivity. Avoid this. Don't compromise your integrity by taking what belongs to others.

9. **Do not lie about others** (2 Peter 2:10-13)
   Do not spread stories about your boss or co-workers at work. Don't gossip, and stay out of company politics.

10. **Be satisfied with what you have** (1 Timothy 6:6-11)
    Be content. Yes, pursue God goals, but wanting more always leads to emotional, financial and spiritual bondage.

MY MONDAY JOURNEY LOG

Journey log starter questions:

1. What is one thing you see most improving on Monday?

    (Ex. your attitudes, decisions, relationships, peace or purpose)

    _____

2. What specifically would you like to see God do this next Monday?

    _____

    _____

3. Who can you pray for at work this week? Did you?

    _____

    _____

MY PRAYERS & NOTES

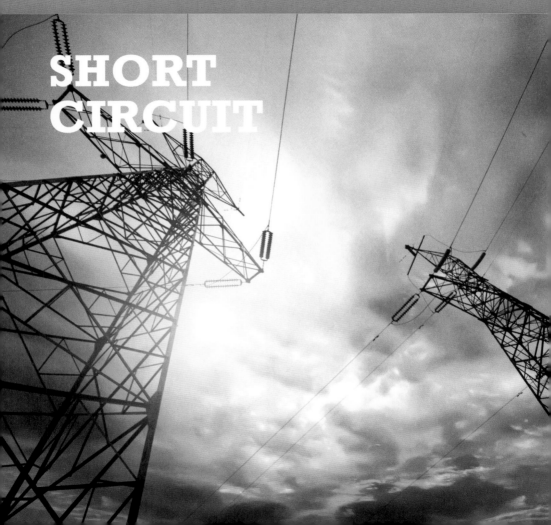

SHORT CIRCUIT

Your Lights Can Go Out!

God created work and created YOU to work. That truth alone can make it easier to keep God switched ON. Unfortunately, there is another belief that can keep you in the dark. It is a short circuit.

Just as a short circuit in a light switch will keep the lights from coming on, a short circuit in your thinking can cause the same thing.

Today, we will unpack a very common spiritual short circuit—the false belief that only *some parts* of life are spiritual. This belief can wreck your ability to Switch God ON at work. So, let's fix it right now!

OVERVIEW

We all want purpose in life and work; but, an all too common belief creates a powerful drain on your purpose. We call this a short circuit. It stops you from switching God ON even if you fully understand that God created work and enjoys it when you work well. It can trap you in Monday Morning Atheism despite your best efforts to escape. This short circuit is the belief that only some parts of life are spiritual.

> *short circuit* (shôrt) def. *the belief that only some parts of life are spiritual.*

A short circuit is something that disrupts proper flow, or in this case, proper understanding. We can miss the main truth or point. Short circuits in our thinking or beliefs are dangerous because they can cause damage to our entire work life. Total spiritual black out happens in some cases. Nobody wants a short circuit showing up on Mondays!

If you allow any semblance of these lies to take root on your Monday, or any day for that matter, you are devaluing the unique talents, skills and purpose God has given to you.

Let's start by thinking about this. Throughout the Bible, workers served God in many forms: farmers, priests, ranchers, carpenters, doctors, tax collectors, temple (church) workers, guards and hundreds of other trades are also mentioned. If you think about it, most jobs we have today were represented in the Bible—we may be more high tech, and mass production oriented, but the jobs are similar.

Stop and think about this. There are so many jobs and so many people—Does God value some jobs more than others? This is a tricky question for most of us. Why is one person purposed for this job and another gifted for that job? Are some jobs more important to God? Confusion about the true value of your work can come from many sources, but one clear cause is the misunderstanding of a common word we often hear used. It is the term "ministry".

Who actually does ministry and what does this mean? Is it exclusive to those who perform certain jobs, like missionaries and pastors? The word "ministry" actually comes from a root word that means "to serve", as in serving God and His people, our neighbors and coworkers. So any job done with God and for His purpose is ministry. We are all involved in service work. When we have the correct understanding of the word "ministry," we realize the common misconception that God thinks some jobs are more spiritual than other jobs is simply not true. If you follow Christ and you work, guess what? You are in ministry!

".... whoever wants to become great among you must be your servant." —Matthew 20:26 (NIV)

Another aspect of this misunderstanding extracts a heavy toll on us. Many believe that life fits into one of two compartments. Either what I am doing is spiritual or my work is normal, common, everyday and thus spiritually unimportant. This is a lie. It may even be rooted in some of our early church experiences, but nonetheless it is a lie, and it is destructive.

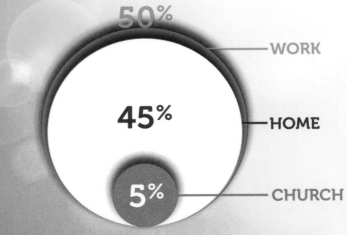

50% — WORK

45% — HOME

5% — CHURCH

We tend to believe that the spiritual aspect of life only involves activities like church (when we actually attend), prayer (when we are in a tight jam), and possibly reading our Bible (if we are really serious). Other spiritual activities, like serving the homeless or short-term missions, may also qualify. Thinking that these types of activities are most important or, worse yet, the only stuff that really matters to God is inconsistent with Biblical truth.

"Whatever you do, do it all for the glory of God"

1 Corinthians 10:31 (NIV)

Do you ever treat your work as if it were unrelated to God? If so, then you've probably struggled with spiritual schizophrenia and the dim and lifeless work that comes with it. Monday Morning Atheism is living with a kind of "spiritual schizophrenia," a case of having a split mind with God and work on opposing sides. This thinking comes from a false belief that life divides neatly into different compartments with only a small part of life being truly spiritual and the rest being non spiritual, or at least spiritually neutral.

(pages 42–45 Monday Morning Atheist, the book)

Without much thought, many of us label what we perceive to be the un-spiritual segments of life as "secular." Did you know that the word secular means "without God"? Here's the problem with that. There is no place on this planet that God does not function. We are not designed to just **do** missions, like a mission trip; we are designed to be on mission everyday, no matter what our particular job might be. In short, real biblical ministry is done by God's people, wherever he has put them or wherever they find themselves. Listen to this amazing encouragement from the Bible:

> *"So here's what I want you to do, God helping you: Take your everyday, ordinary life—your sleeping, eating, going-to-work and walking around life—and place it before God as an offering."* —Romans 12:1 (The Message)

So we're starting to see that this idea of only some types of work being spiritual is badly flawed. It denies the biblical truth that everything in creation was made by God and for His glory. "For in Him all things were created: things in heaven and on earth, visible and invisible, whether thrones or powers or rulers or authorities; all things have been creat-ed through Him and for Him" Colossians 1:16 (NIV). Everything in the

world, everything in your life—it is all His. In Psalms 139:7 it says "Where shall I go from thy spirit? Where shall I flee from thy presence?"

> *"In the total expanse of human life there is not a single square inch of which the Christ, who alone is sovereign, does not declare, 'That is mine!'*
> —Abraham Kuyper

So, Sundays are not more spiritual than Monday! Mondays are not "just work" with Sundays being the really spiritual days. Jesus did not devote his ministry exclusively to Sunday (or Saturday); more often, Jesus spent most of his time and told most of his stories on Monday or a work day. Imagine if, every Sunday, millions of Christians would exit the church knowing their mission field is just outside those church doors—and they refused to Switch OFF their faith on Monday! Every day belongs to God. Your work is valuable to God no matter the day of the week.

The work you do on Monday is important to your Heavenly Father. He created you and he knows you better than anyone. He has uniquely designed you and strategically placed you to represent Him in the workplace. He set you apart, for what He needs done right now, right here. Your work is ministry! God says in the Bible: Before I formed you in the womb I knew you, before you were born I set you apart... Jeremiah 1:5 (NIV)

Our work is often referred to as a "vocation." The word "vocation" comes from the Latin word "vocare" which means "to call". As if God is actually calling you to work. Your vocation is wherever you apply the aptitude, talent, or ability that God has given you. Our society is more impressed with some jobs than others, but our God does not feel the same way. He is more impressed about how we do our job and if we are doing it with Him or without Him.

God created you with your own attributes, your own unique DNA! You did not select your attributes any more than you chose your eye color. Your gifts and talents are no more or less valuable than the next person, no matter their spiritual status or your role at work. You only get to choose what you are going to do with your talents. The key to real success at work has little to do with which job you have or what talents you have: it has much more to do with choosing God first and doing the best you can. Your real job is to use your God-given gifts to the best of your ability, right where you are.

God desires to help you and bless you as you work. He wants you to thrive. Do not settle for less than that which you were made for. You were created uniquely to do special work in God's eyes. Switch God ON and fully experience His joy in your work! ⏻

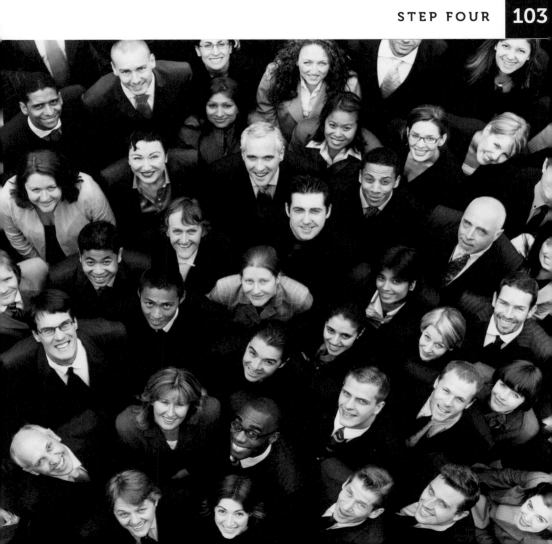

MONDAY MOAN METER (CHECK IN)

LET'S STOP AND THINK ABOUT THIS PAST MONDAY

Mark your Moan Time now.
Circle your Moan Time on the Monday Moan Meter to the right.

Discuss with Others:
What triggered your initial feelings of moan this past Monday?

....

MY MONDAY CHECK-IN:

done?

- [ ] **I COMPLETED** my "Work is GOOD" Actions (listed in Step3)

- [ ] **I READ** STEP FOUR Overview

- [ ] **Work 10 Commandments** – I posted/sent to a friend

- [ ] **I SHOUTED** "Work is Good" 7 times on last Monday.

- [ ] **MONDAY JOURNEY LOG** - I logged my experience.

MOAN: *def. verb* - to grumble, whine, complain, groan, or gripe either in thought or word.

SHOWTIME (FEATURE VIDEO)

In today's Showtime we will explore the possibility of "Your Work being your real Ministry". Really? Yes. Let's start Step 4 video now.

Consider: Have you ever felt like Jill, the school teacher in this video? You know—Sunday vs Monday or spiritual work vs "regular" work?

Share: When have you felt this same way? Share with your group.

You are designed to be ON mission—every day.

Any job done with God and for His purposes is real ministry".

"*My work is important to God*"
#MondaySwitch

WORKING IT OUT (GOING DEEPER)

Whether washing a car, designing a building or any of a thousand other jobs—God designed you to represent Him in the workplace.

EVERYONE:
QUICKLY RAISE YOUR HAND IF YOU ARE IN FULL TIME MINISTRY. GO!

If you did not raise your hand—what percent of your time is in ministry? _____% ⓪─25─50─75─100

What do you do in your "non-ministry time"? Honestly, is your work/job what you consider "non-ministry time"? DISCUSS this with group:

_____

_____

SOMEONE READ THIS OUTLOUD:
"MINISTRY" comes from a root word meaning "to serve"—as in serving God, your family, your company, and your co-workers.

EACH PERSON IN YOUR GROUP:

List 2 ways that you recently did "Ministry" through your work (Hint: it is not just spiritual activities—Jesus built furniture):

_____

_____

Q: Have you ever felt that God might be more pleased if you had a more "spiritual job"?

What would that job be? _____

Would a new job really be more spiritual? Share with Group.

WE SEEM TO CATEGORIZE JOBS AND TALENTS:

God does not. He has gifted you and wired you uniquely different from anyone else. List ONE personality or character attribute about you that is very unique. Then share it with your group.

Attribute: _____

Q: Are you using your unique attribute in the workplace to help further God's kingdom in some way? If so, how?"

"THE SWITCH" WORK PRAYER

Find the "The Switch" Work Prayer at the end of this session. Someone volunteer to read this prayer boldly to bless the entire group. *Wow! Can you imagine praying this prayer every day at work!*

Q: What part of this prayer especially speaks truth to your heart right now? Share this.

GOD'S INSTRUCTIONS

someone read this to group: "So here's what I want you to do, God helping you: Take your everyday, ordinary life—your sleeping, eating, going-to-work and walking around life—and place it before God as an offering." Romans 12:1 (The Message)

Q: Regarding this verse, do you see any part of your life that is excluded from God's instructions here? Discuss

---

Somebody in
your group needs
personal prayer.

Who is it?

Pray for them
right now.

SWITCH IT ON (PRACTICAL STEPS)

Let's make some serious progress this week on blocking this short circuit. You are going to love the next step in this process.

....

MY MONDAY MUST-DOS:

(Go to MondaySwitch.com/STEP4)

 THE SWITCH WORK PRAYER (on next page) and at MondaySwitch.com/Step4. Pray this each work day until next Monday. Post on Twitter & FB each day "I've prayed my work prayer today #MondaySwitch" to encourage others in your group.

DOWNLOAD and READ a short, insightful section of the book, Monday Morning Atheist called *Spiritual Schizophrenia*—go to MondaySwitch.com/Step4

 My MONDAY JOURNEY LOG—spend a few minutes before next session and log how Mondays are going.

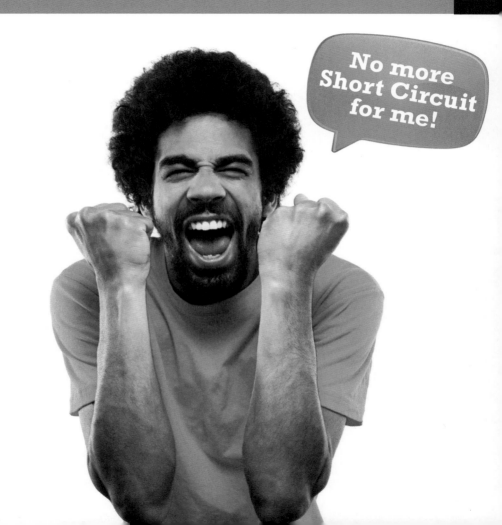

THE SWITCH WORK PRAYER

(download, post or print at MondaySwitch.com/Step4)

Lord Jesus, as I begin my work, I bring Your presence with me. I speak Your peace, Your grace and Your perfect order into the atmosphere of my work.

I acknowledge Your Lordship over all that will be spoken, thought, decided and accomplished this day.

Lord Jesus, I thank you for the gifts and skills You have deposited in me. I do not take them lightly, but commit to using them responsibly and well.

Give me a fresh supply of truth and beauty on which to draw as I do my job today. Bless my creativity, my ideas,

my energy so that even my smallest task may bring You honor.

Lord, when I'm confused, guide me—when I'm weary, energize me.

Lord, when I'm burned out, infuse me with the light of Your Holy Spirit.

May the work I do and the way I do it bring hope, life, and courage to all that I come into contact with today.

And oh Lord, even in this day's most stressful moments, may I rest in You.

In the name of Jesus, I pray. Amen. ⏻

MY MONDAY JOURNEY LOG

Journey log starter questions:

1. What is one thing you see most improving on Monday?

    (Ex. your attitudes, decisions, relationships, peace or purpose)

    _____

2. What specifically would you like to see God do this next Monday?

    _____

    _____

3. Who can you pray for at work this week? Did you?

    _____

    _____

MY PRAYERS & NOTES

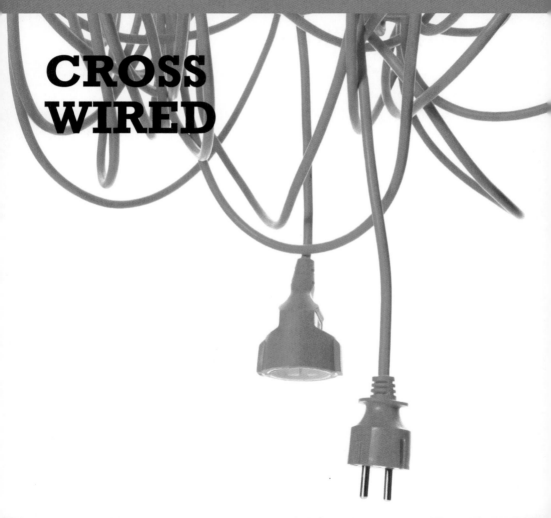

CROSS WIRED

Working WITH God on Monday!

Have you ever put on a pair of drugstore glasses or tried on someone else's eye glasses? Things can really look strange! The same can happen if you are not looking through the correct spiritual lens, the one provided by God to see clearly and accurately.

Too often we struggle with a view of ourselves that falls far short of how God sees us—a view that is not in alignment with who we really are.

You are about to discover a new perspective—a clear vision of yourself that will change your work on Monday. The big idea for this session is "I am working WITH God". Transformation to your work is coming!

OVERVIEW

The human eye is one of God's most complex wonders! Although we can function without sight, we rely heavily on vision to live our everyday lives! We depend on our eyes more than any other sense. Our eyes are composed of more than two million parts, all working together. And they can process 36,000 bits of information every hour.

The human eye makes it possible to see your physical world with clarity, but the way you see yourself goes well beyond what your physical eyes see.

In fact, your perspective is one of the most powerful tools you have for success in life: but, this requires that you see things differently. Your emotional and spiritual perspectives shape your life. If you hope to grow—to work differently—you must first correct your vision in order to see yourself through a clear lens, more like God does.

By now, you're beginning to see Mondays differently, right? But, in order to stay Switched ON for God you have to see yourself as you really are—through God's eyes! From His perspective! Think about this, when Jesus exchanged His life for your life, you were in essence wired to the Cross of Jesus. That's remarkable! Put another way, you are now CROSSwired because of Him! Your true identity and your ability to

thrive come from this position of perspective and power. And listen to this—how you perceive or feel does not change this fact! This is who God says you are. It is simply the truth.

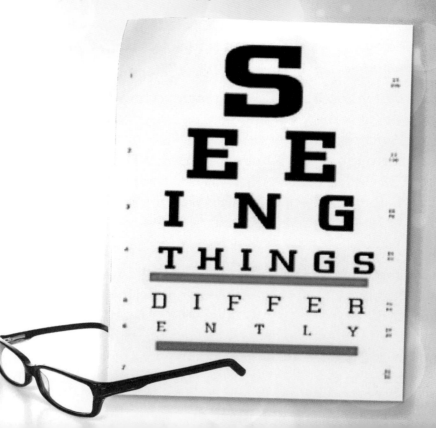

As a follower of Christ, your character, your source of power, and your work itself changed because of the Cross of Jesus. So being CROSS-wired means you can WORK from this position of authority—it's who you really are. If you don't know who you really are at work, it doesn't matter how many times you Switch God ON—the power will quickly start to flicker and eventually switch OFF. None of us want that to happen over and over again!

FACT: Your view of yourself is the driving force to how you approach your Monday work. It is most common for people to work WITHOUT God, alone and switched OFF. Yet sometimes—while trying to switch ON—work can seem like an even heavier burden. Without knowing it, we try to work FOR God as the boss: basically thinking, "I have to do this myself FOR God". But God desires another way, a much better way—Working WITH God—trusting Him, resting in His ways, and therefore working WITH Him.

Let's take a moment and consider another of God's workers, Noah. Noah arguably had one of the most challenging of all work projects—the Ark. For over 50 years he had to be faithful, diligent, and precise while he worked on the Ark. He also had to put up with lots of workplace harassment and ridicule, while continuing to trust in God. Despite all this, the bible says in Gen 6:9 that Noah was a just man, and Noah walked WITH God.

Similar to Noah, to experience meaning and purpose in our work we need to focus on working WITH God. Working WITH God means working from your true identity, and from the new life God gave you. 2 Corinthians 5:15 says "He died for everyone so that those who receive his new life will no longer live for themselves." Remember, to grow close to God, you must learn to work WITH God on Monday!

Long term personal fulfillment comes from partnering WITH God, truly working WITH God. In fact, either you work from the truth of being CROSSwired OR you work from a distorted perspective that traps you in a form of Monday Morning Atheism—working like God does not exist.

Please receive this truth: you are never, ever alone. God exists, and He is with you. Until we realize that God is with us when we are working, we will not be freed from Monday Morning Atheism. Until then, we will always struggle to have meaning and life in our work. (page 74 Monday Morning Atheist, the book)

We can work WITH God and depend solely on Him. Listen to how He cares for us: "Don't panic. I'm with you. There's no need to fear for I'm your God. I'll give you strength. I'll help you. I'll hold you steady, keep a firm grip on you. Isaiah 41:10 (MSG)

WORK **WITHOUT** GOD

Alone   *Switched off*

Isolated   *Independent*

Lonely   *Monday Morning Atheist*

WORK **FOR** GOD

Doing more   *Duty*

Trying hard   *Pleasing God & man*

Perform better

WORK **WITH** GOD

Diligent   *Relating*   *Talking*   *Obeying*

Resting   *Enjoying*

Peace

Of course, most of us attempt to Switch God ON at work but accidently fall into the trap of working FOR God instead of WITH God. Working FOR God seems great at first but quickly becomes stressful as you push yourself to perform for God much like you would for an employer.

Working FOR God in this manner is not what God's grace is all about! If you work trying to earn acceptance, your switch will slowly slide to a dimmer setting and eventually go completely OFF. Stay Switched ON. CROSSwired. Receive God's free gift of grace and the power that comes with it.

Working WITHOUT God has numerous negative outcomes as we learned in prior sessions. Here are two common ones for quick review.

1. Your work can quickly become an idol. You work too much. You can't stop. Your priorities get out of whack. You become a workaholic.

    Or just the opposite occurs.

2. You develop a complete disregard for work. This "forget it" attitude is a slippery slope to a form of laziness that God detests.

In either case, an ongoing life of self-reliance can suck the life and joy from your work.

As you work WITH God He promises to GO before you each day. He precedes you in that work situation, that decision, that relationship.

It is God's grace that gets to work first! Isaiah 52:12 says "For the Lord will go ahead of you; yes, the God of Israel will protect you from behind." God's nature and goodness actually goes before you in your life and work. That's incredible, isn't it? You can rest, trusting that God anticipates and gets there first.

His divine power has given us everything we need for a godly life through our knowledge of him who called us by his own glory and goodness. —2 Peter 1:3

In thinking about staying switched ON we can hold on to another incredible truth. The Bible says that you and I already have everything we need to work WITH God. You do not need to search, beg or attain anything else. It is IN you, WITH you, GIVEN to you. 2 Peter 1:3 promises: "His divine power has given us everything we need for a godly life through our knowledge of him who called us by his own glory and goodness.

Did you hear that? EVERYTHING you need—not some things—EVERYTHING!

"I'm working WITH God from now on!"
#MondaySwitch

The one essential goal of this session is to understand that you are accepted and loved by God and built to work WITH Him for his glory. You cannot make God happier by performing better in any way. YES—Being faithful and diligent at work is important. But, there is no need or use in performing out of compulsion or a desire to please God or any person.

What if Christ, for the believer, is never over there, on the other side of our sin? What if the power of His death on the cross allows Him to stand right in front of me, on my worst day and smile bigger and happier than any human being ever could? This life in Christ is not about what I can do to make myself worthy of His acceptance, but about daily trusting what He has done to make me worthy of His acceptance. He wants us to learn dependence on Him instead of performance. We're learning to trust His power in us. The beauty is, we actually fail less in doing so.

God has given us the DNA of righteousness. We are saints. Nothing we do will make us more righteous than we already are. Nothing we do will alter this reality. God knows our DNA. He knows that we are "Christ in me". And now He is asking us to join Him in what He knows is true! From the book, The Cure

You can work with great hope, anticipation and joy knowing that God knows your DNA is "In Christ." You are accepted just as you are. God not only loves you but really likes you. And when you are tired, stressed or overwhelmed, God has a strategy to help you work WITH Him. In Jesus' own words "Come to me, all of you who are tired from carrying heavy loads, and I will give you rest." Matthew 11:28 (GNT).

Let's keep the corrected vision of who we are because of the cross of Jesus. This perspective affects our attitudes and actions; and it makes all the difference on Mondays. Every day declare who you really are! You are CROSSwired. You have the mind of Christ and you are God's prized possession created to do good works WITH Him. ⏻

MONDAY MOAN METER (CHECK IN)

IT'S HARD TO MOAN WITH A GRATEFUL HEART!

Mark your Moan Time now.
Circle your Moan Time on the Monday Moan Meter to the right.

Discuss in Group:
Did your Moan Time come down this past Monday? Why or why not?

. . . .

MY MONDAY CHECK IN:

☐ **I READ STEP** FIVE Overview.

☐ **I PRAYED "The Switch Prayer" each Day.**
I placed it where I can see it. I posted on FB & Twitter.

☐ **Monday Morning Atheist**—I downloaded the FREE section.

☐ **MONDAY JOURNEY LOG**—I logged my experience.

MOAN: *def. verb* - to grumble, whine, complain, groan, or gripe either in thought or word.

SHOWTIME (FEATURE VIDEO)

Get ready for some powerful truth here. The big idea this session is about Working WITH God. Someone start the video now.

Try This: Wow, did you feel that truth about yourself? As a group—raise both your hands. Go ahead—as high as you can and say together slowly: "I am who God says I am!"

Share: What did you feel inside during the "I am CROSSwired" segment in the video? What if you really lived from that truth?.

God likes you!

You are accepted and loved by Go

Built to work WITH Him on Monda

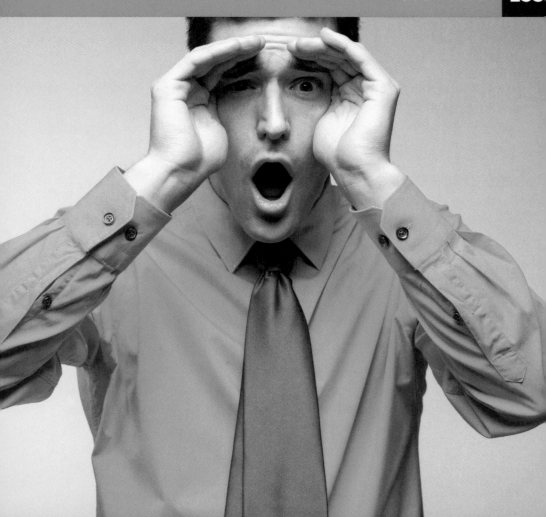

WORKING IT OUT (GOING DEEPER)

When Jesus exchanged His life for your life, you were in essence wired to the Cross of Jesus—CROSSwired. "He died for everyone, so that those who receive his new life will no longer live for themselves..." 2 Corinthians 5:15 (GNT)

READ THIS VERSE OUT LOUD:
His divine power has given us everything we need for a godly life through our knowledge of him who called us by his own glory and goodness. 2 Peter 1:3 (NIV)

Q: "everything we need"—Are you missing anything needed to live a Godly life? Discuss.

_____

_____

Q: Why do you think we so frequently turn to someone or something instead of trusting and using what we already have? Discuss.

_____

_____

NOAH WORKED WITH GOD

For over 50 years Noah worked on building the ark to God's specs. That is a long time to stay on task at work! Especially while being jeered for believing God. Even so, Noah continued working WITH God!

Q: What would it have taken for you to stay focused and work WITH God under these work circumstances? Discuss.

COMMONLY WE APPROACH WORK IN ONE OF 3 WAYS:

What about you? Mark what % of time you spend working in each approach during a work week?

You work WITHOUT God _____% of week

You work FOR God _____% of week

You work WITH God _____% of week

Share This Together.

Working WITH God requires that you see yourself as God sees you. Share a time at work in which you worked WITH God to accomplish a task or project:

MY IDENTITY – CROSSWIRED (GROUP EXERCISE)

You are now CROSSwired because of Jesus, loved and accepted completely. This is remarkable! This is the way to work WITH God!

#1 READ:

Someone read to the group... Turn to the "CROSSwired" declaration page at back of this Step and read the declaration aloud to the group.

#2 CHOOSE :

While this is being read, listen to God. CIRCLE 3 truths that inspire you most. Maybe it's those that need reinforcment in your life and work.

#3 DISCUSS:

Discuss these questions with your group.

Q: Why did you choose these particular truths? Any specific reasons? Share with others.

Q: What do you think blocks people, and specifically you from fully receiving God's view of who you are and what He feels about you? Discuss this together.

Q: "God does for you what you cannot do for yourself" How does this statement strike you? Discuss.

#4 PRAY:

As a group, close your eyes and sit in silence for ONE minute and privately ask God for His help in seeing His truth about you. Thank Him for what He has done for you!

SWITCH IT ON (PRACTICAL STEPS)

This is a really important step in the process—working from who we are in Christ. Let's make sure this sinks in during this next work week.

....

MY MONDAY MUST-DOS:

(Go to MondaySwitch.com/STEP5)

☐ **THE "CROSSwired" DECLARATION**

Go To www.mondayswitch.com/Step5 and download.

- Repeat this declaration out loud on Mondays.
- Share it with 3 co-workers or friends. #MondaySwitch

☐ **SAY "I AM WHO GOD SAYS I AM"** as loud as you can on your way to work next Monday.

☐ **WITH GOD:** On your next work day, pause before each decision that day and say, "God, You are WITH me—let's do this together".

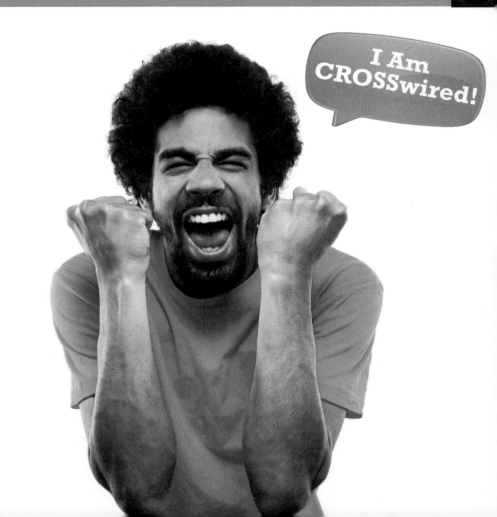

"CROSSWIRED" DECLARATION

(share, post or print at MondaySwitch.com/Step5)

I AM CROSSWIRED

I am the most stunning and valuable of all God's creation. I am changed by the Cross of Jesus. I am powerful, strong and capable at work. I am unique. I have potential. And God says my work is GOOD!

I AM CROSSWIRED

I am a new creation. I am a child of the Most High God. I am highly favored and freely accepted. My God is always working—and I am made in His likeness. I have amazing qualities, traits and skill. I am full of power, strength, and determination.

⚡ I AM CROSSWIRED

I am God's masterpiece—His prized possession. I am His work-manship created to do good works. I am loved despite my mistakes. I have the mind of Christ. He empowers me at work. He goes before me at work. Nothing I face is too much for me—I am an overcomer!

⚡ I AM CROSSWIRED

I am sent by God to work. I co-labor with Christ. I have talents and skills to share. I am an artist, a leader, an inventor, a builder, a technician—My talents can change my world and those around me. God has planned my work ahead of time. I work WITH God.

⚡ I AM CROSSWIRED

I thank God for Mondays! He has made me ready for every good work. I have everything I need to thrive. I carry God's presence with me daily. What I can't do for myself—He does for me. He works all things out for my good. I am cherished and loved. I am FREE! I am—who God says I am!!!

MY MONDAY JOURNEY LOG

Journey log starter questions:

1. What is one thing you see most improving on Monday?

   (Ex. your attitudes, decisions, relationships, peace or purpose)

   _____

2. What specifically would you like to see God do this next Monday?

   _____

   _____

3. Who can you pray for at work this week? Did you?

   _____

   _____

MY PRAYERS & NOTES

MPOWERED

I'm Powered by God for Monday!

Wow! This is our last session together. But for you—it is just the START of a whole new way of working on Mondays.

Your vision of who God says you are is now sharpened, and you are now learning to work WITH God more consistently.

We will now discover the power that God has placed inside you to accomplish your work, and to transform your Mondays. So let's start by Thanking God for Mondays and then upgrading to His power source.

OVERVIEW

It was the 1924 Olympics and a runner named Eric Liddell inspired millions. Preparing for his race, he was taunted by fellow competitors who felt sure he would lose, especially because he ran in a race earlier that day. Just as Eric stepped to the start line, an American Olympic Team member slipped a piece of paper into his hand that said "in the Bible it says: 'he that honors Me, I will honor.'" Eric grasped the note and asked himself, "So where will the power in me come from—to finish this race?" He quickly answered himself: "I believe God made me for a purpose. He made me fast and I'm going to run for His pleasure." Eric ran WITH God—powered by God—and won the Olympic 400 meter race.

There are 3 important takeaways from Eric's story: First and most important: **There is a power inside you, freely given to you by God, to accomplish your work.** Second: Like Eric, **God made you for a purpose—an assignment.** For most of us, this is our work—our vocation. And finally, **If you honor God—He will honor you.** You can count on this! God has given you His power so you have capacity well beyond what you can do on your own!

So, as a follower of Christ, what is the purpose for this power?

pow·er n. The ability or capacity to perform or act effectively.

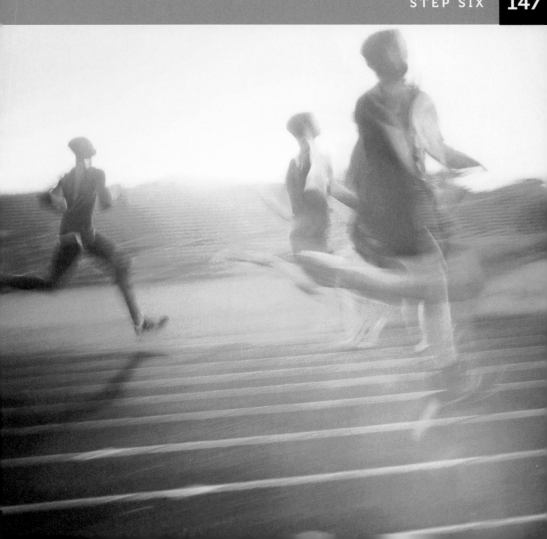

One definition of pow·er (pou r) n. is the ability or capacity to perform or act effectively. No matter what your job or profession, the desire to act and perform effectively is natural. Your desire to be productive is not only for your own good but also for the good of others and your family.

However, to be your best you will absolutely need God's power. His power produces the strength, the stamina, the creativity, and the gumption to run your race well!

You see, God called Eric Liddell to run fast: and, fueled with the power of God, Eric responded. And so it is with you. God's Spirit literally empowers you for work on Monday.

We call this: "M"powered—("Monday") Powered—powered by God for Mondays! God has freely given you His power to accomplish your work, to thrive in ways that would otherwise not be possible. The concept of thriving means flourishing at work, doing well, and succeeding while bringing glory to God. You are Mpowered by God to work this way every Monday. To Thrive!

Too often our view of God is too small. In this way, we limit His power within us. We need to reflect and ask "How Big is my God?" For a little perspective on God's power consider this, the sun and its power were created by God's hand. You can fit 1.3 million Earths inside the Sun.

The temperature inside the Sun can reach 15 million degrees Celsius. At the sun's core, power is generated by nuclear fusion, as Hydrogen converts to Helium. Because hot objects generally expand, the Sun would explode like a giant bomb if it weren't for its enormous gravitational force. Here is the wild part: that same potential power—God's power—which created the sun and the entire universe is the same power that is inside of you! The Bible refers to God's power as the Holy Spirit. As a believer He lives inside of you.

Because of this power (the Holy Spirit inside of you), you are promised in the Bible that you do not need to rely on your own batteries. On Mondays you can rely on God. You are powered by God for Monday!

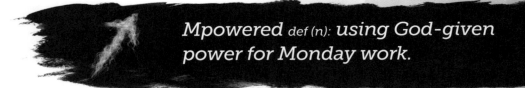

Mpowered def (n): using God-given power for Monday work.

We can do all the work in the world repairing the short circuits of our beliefs, making sure that we've patched over lies with truth, but if we're not plugged into the ultimate power source, the lights won't stay on. Real change in our life begins when we plug into God—specifically, the Holy Spirit, who is our source of strength. Without that connection we are essen-

tially powerless, destined to work in the dark. The Holy Spirit is the power grid—the true and abundant source of power needed for running things in our life, for making changes to our character, and for keeping the lights on in our work life.

(pg. 104-105 Monday Morning Atheist, the book)

What will it take for you to stay Switched ON—to access this power to work on Mondays consistently? It requires staying in the moment with God—keeping God at the top of your mind and allowing Him to influence each moment of your work and life. You do this by checking your Switch frequently, pushing the Power button ON, then checking and pushing it again if needed. Stay at it and this will become more natural—a habit!

Keeping His presence your priority at work is essential. FACT: you can do nothing of significance without Him. Listen to Jesus "I am the vine, and you are the branches. Those who remain in me, and I in them, will bear much fruit; for you can do nothing without me. John 15:5 (GNT)

"I have appointed you for the very purpose of displaying my power in you and to spread my fame throughout the earth." —Romans 9:17 (NLT)

As we come to the end of our time together, ask yourself, "Why has God given me His power to accomplish my work?" Why is it so critical that I stay Switched ON? What is it? Why do it?

It can't be just to work harder, to work better or to give more. Yes, these things are important, but what is the central purpose for God's power in your life? Let's look at the Bible for one of these answers: "I have appointed you for the very purpose of displaying my power in you and to spread my fame throughout the earth." Romans 9:17 (NLT)

When your feet hit the ground Monday morning, say "Ok God—this is Your Monday and Your work. So, let's go to work."

Stop for a moment and breathe this in! You have been appointed to display God's power. The word "appointed" has a significant meaning as you GO into your work on Monday. It literally means prearranged, decided, agreed upon, determined, assigned and established. God has prearranged your life and work: then sends you on assignment. As His representative, you are sent as an ambassador! You carry the full power and authority of Jesus as you go and accomplish your work on this earth.

Being sent by God as an ambassador is similar to a foreign ambassador who represents his country abroad. In the same way, you are sent to represent Jesus *where you are*. You are equipped and resourced for your assignment—and never left alone or expected to do it by yourself! God sends you with a capacity that extends well beyond what you could do on your own. You go Mpowered with unique talents and influence to change your world—displaying God's power and making Him known. Now that is quite the job description!

Romans 12:2 says: "Let God change your life. First of all, let Him give you a new mind. Then you will know what God wants you to do. And the things you do will be good and pleasing and perfect." Go to work on Mondays with gratitude and in such a way that people observe you living the right way. Make moral, ethical and wise decisions; staying away from gossip; and demonstrating Godly character. When you live

this way, and when people see the inner peace and joy of a Switched ON life, amazing things happen. For 52 Mondays a year we have the privilege of being a significant part of The Switch revolution—living Switched ON for God. Along with millions of others, we stand together proclaiming "Monday is for God's glory!"

Switch God ON and GO Live It and Share It! "Thank God it's Monday"

MONDAY MOAN METER (CHECK IN)

WE KNOW YOU ARE LEAVING "MOAN-DAY" BEHIND. THIS IS OUR LAST MOAN TIME CHECK IN. CONGRATULATIONS.

Mark your Moan Time again.
Circle your Moan Time on the Monday Moan Meter to the right?

LOOK BACK and Compare:
Let's record what your Moan Time is now compared to the start.

....

RECORD (TIME):
This Week's Moan Time: _____

Moan Time at Start:_____

DISCUSS:
What is the difference in your Moan Time from the start until now?
What are the main reasons for your change?

WHAT'S YOUR MOAN TIME?

1 HRS 2HRS 3HRS 4HRS 5HRS 6HRS

Monday Moan Meter

MOAN: *def. verb* - to grumble, whine, complain, groan, or gripe either in thought or word.

SHOWTIME (FEATURE VIDEO)

Okay, TGIM! You are powered by God for so much more. Let's find out how we stay Switched ON. Start Step 6 video.

Find Out: Who is the fastest runner in the room? Pick somebody now.

Fastest Runner: Share one thing that has changed in you on Mondays since we started this journey.

Group Share: What work situation do you need God's power for right now—to run with endurance? Share it.

You possess the full power and authority of Jesus as you GO and accomplish your work on this earth.

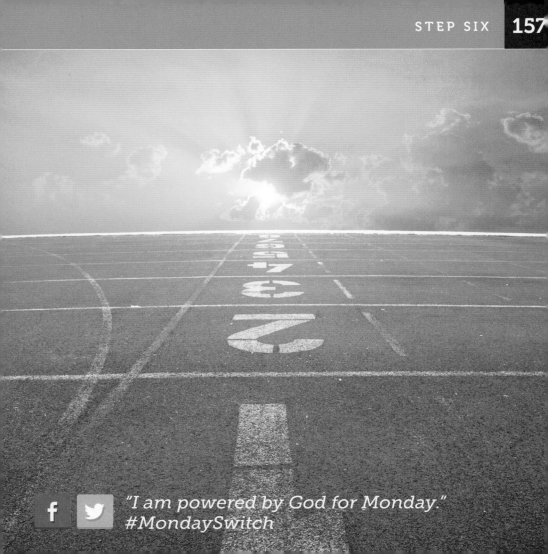

"I am powered by God for Monday."
#MondaySwitch

WORKING IT OUT (GOING DEEPER)

There is a power inside you, freely given to you by God, to accomplish your work. It is a power that gives you capacity well beyond what you could ever do on your own.

SOMEONE READ OUT-LOUD:
"I have appointed you for the very purpose of displaying My power in you and to spread My fame throughout the earth." Romans 9:17

Amazingly, as a Christ follower you have the same power (Holy Spirit) inside you that raised Jesus from the dead—the same power that heals and does miracles.

Q: How can knowing this truth affect the way you approach work on Monday?

SHARE WITH YOUR GROUP:

THINK ABOUT THIS

Write your last two jobs in the spaces below.

Job One:_____

Job Two:_____

Share:

In those jobs, did you see God's power at work in you to accomplish what you could not? **How? Give an example. If not, why do you think so?**

_____

_____

ERIC LIDDELL SAID:

"I believe God made me for a purpose. He made me fast and I'm going to run for His pleasure."

Q: Can you remember a time that you seriously felt God's pleasure when you worked? When was that? Discuss this with group.

_____

_____

SENT INTO THE (WORK) WORLD:
(Someone read this to the group):

Jesus himself prayed directly to His Father for you in John 17:15-18:

"My prayer is not that you take them out of the world but that you protect them... As You sent Me into the world, I have sent them into the world."

Right from the mouth of Jesus He said you are SENT into the world. And that means work for most of us.

Group Discuss:
How does Jesus' words change your thinking on Mondays?

SHARE WITH GROUP:
What specific things have you learned that will change Mondays and your view of work from now on?

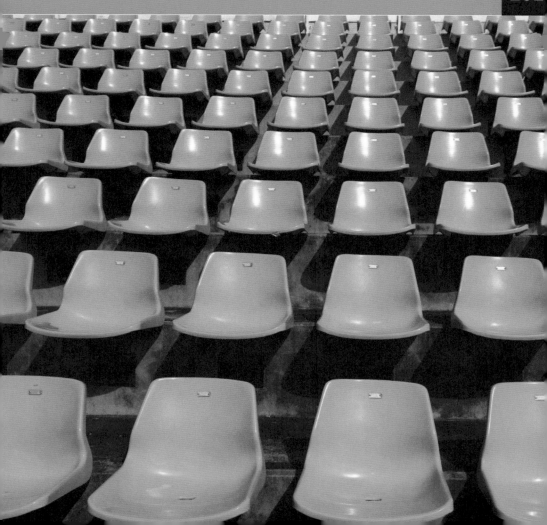

THE "MOAN-LESS MONDAY" PLEDGE

We have made a lot of changes together during The Switch. Someone read the "Moan-less Monday" Pledge below.

Q: **Can each of you commit to this personally?**

(If so, each of you sign this pledge as a group.)

Dear God,

I have made The Switch to keep you ON each Monday. I pledge not to moan on Mondays but to instead grow in my ability to see my work as yours. I know that it is You who sends me and gives me the power to stay Switched ON Monday.

Signature _____

Date _____

NEXT 21
"NO-MOAN MONDAYS"
CHECKLIST

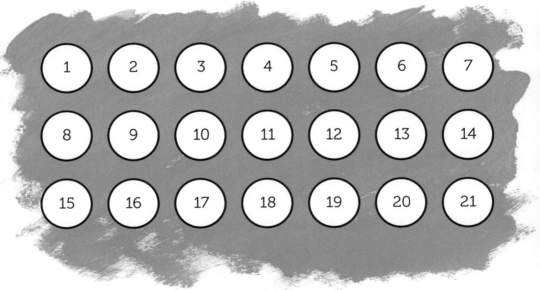

Download Pledge and 21 Mondays Checklist at: MondaySwitch.com/Step6

SWITCH IT ON (PRACTICAL STEPS)

You are being sent with power into Mondays now. Do these final tasks to finish strong.

MY MONDAY MUST-DOS:

(Go to MondaySwitch.com/STEP6)

 SHARE YOUR STORY
Help Spread the Monday Revolution. Share what God has done on your favorite social network. (See Next Page) #MondaySwitch

 AFTER SIGNING THE "MOAN-less Monday" Pledge—DOWNLOAD THE 21 Mondays Check sheet at MondaySwitch.com/Step6. Don't Go back to moaning.

DON'T SWITCH OFF—For more ongoing creative tools for work and Mondays be sure to visit WorkLife.org

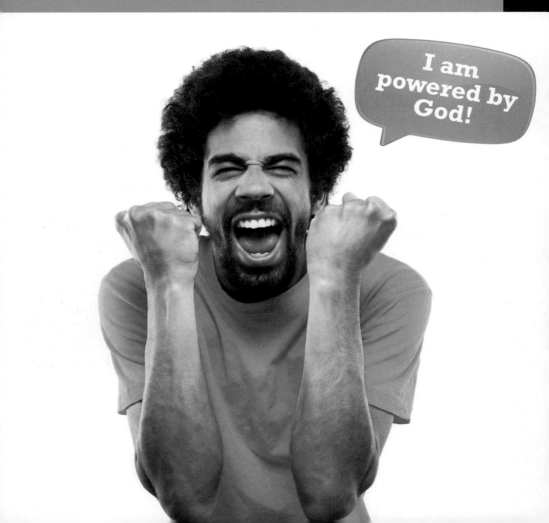

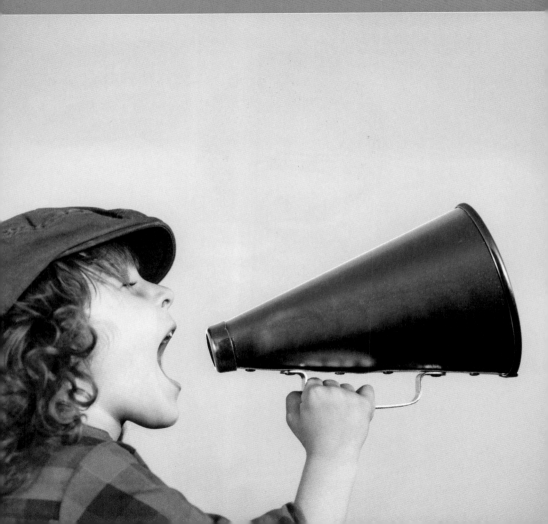

SPREAD GOD'S FAME!

SHARE YOUR STORY

Your Monday Switch will change someone's work and life!

Use hashtag: #MondaySwitch

MondaySwitch.com

MY PRAYERS & NOTES

ABOUT OUR RESEARCH

This book is the product of ten years of research and field experience. We began this project by compiling thirty specific behavioral indicators that measure the integration of faith into everyday issues and key relationships at work. Over the last several years, we have presented this Index of On-the-Job Spiritual Health Indicators to over 5,000 Christians.

Combining census surveying of church congregations with opt-in online participation of individuals, more than 250,000 specific data points have been collected. The respondents compose a non-probability sample, but represent a highly diverse demographic profile in terms of age, gender, ethnicity, Christian faith traditions, vocational pursuits, and geography. The Index itself was crafted with the assistance of Christian experts, who helped us identify the thirty indicators that are the focus of the research.

The collected data spawned the book Monday Morning Atheist which addresses three false assumptions causing Christians to Switch God OFF at work. The SWITCH Six-Step Series provides an experiential journey to help people find God's power in their Monday work.

ABOUT THE AUTHOR

DOUG SPADA

Doug's passion is helping people "Thrive at Work." He is the founder and CEO of WorkLife where he develops innovative resources to help people experience God while they work. Drawing from his unique professional and military background, Doug also speaks internationally on God's plan and purpose for our work, as well as the church's role in that plan.

As a decorated Navy veteran, he served during the Cold War onboard US Navy fast–attack nuclear submarines. He was an instructor at the Navy's top–secret nuclear training facility at the Idaho National Engineering Laboratory. Doug has received numerous commendations during his career, including an Admiral's Citation and the Navy Achievement Medal. In addition to his education in engineering, Doug has a degree in Business Organizational Management. He ran an energy consulting firm in southern California. Doug lives in Atlanta, GA, with Tricia, his wife, and their sons, Ryan and Brayden.

In his book, "Monday Morning Atheist", Doug created a persuasive case based on research about why Christians switch God off at work and how to fix it.

For speaking opportunities or to contact Doug: info@worklife.org

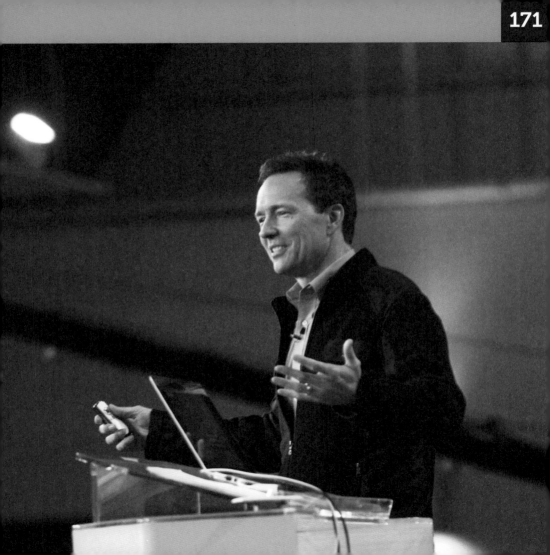

ACKNOWLEDGMENTS

To Tricia, my friend and wife, I love you. I am inspired by the way you work in the medical field with God switched ON. To my sons, Ryan and Brayden, your dad is so proud of you. Always live and work with God switched ON. To my mom and late dad, Lee and Wanda Spada, thank you for loving God and starting me on my faith journey. Thank you to Rusty Gordon for your friendship and service—it is so appreciated. Appreciation for all those who helped this book come alive, especially Jason and Doug at Crosssection Ventures. A huge thanks to Ginger Johnson, my friend and coworker for over a decade. This project would not have been possible without your help and writing. I am so blessed by you. Thanks to all my coworkers throughout the years at WorkLife; you also pursued the dream of inspiring people to follow God at work. Most importantly, to my God and supernatural friend, thank you for giving me Your Spirit and life that produces all good things in me. You amaze me!

"Jesus said to him, 'I am the way, and the truth, and the life; no one comes to the Father but through Me.'" (John 14:6)

ETERNAL JOB SECURITY

When Jesus walked the earth, He was in the business of transforming lives. He invited everyone He encountered to exchange their self-sufficient way of living for a new life in Him. And that offer is still valid today. (Read John 1:12.)

Your very life and even your work are rescued exclusively through Jesus and the power of the Holy Spirit; God has sent His Spirit to be with you forever and unite you with Jesus Christ so that you might become a part of His kingdom for eternity. (Read John 17:3.)

TELL GOD: I can't rescue even a day of my work…let alone my life for all eternity! I need you, Jesus Christ—to do this for me. (Read Isaiah 53:6a.)

Jesus, rescue me personally as I receive Your offer of Light and Life into my spirit. I believe You died on a cross for my sins and I open the door of my life and receive You as my Savior and Lord. (Read John 3:16.)

Thank You for forgiving me, giving me eternal life, and giving me Your Holy Spirit to empower and direct my life and work from this moment forward. (Read Ephesians 2:8–10.)

WORKLIFE
THRIVE AT WORK... EVERYDAY

About WorkLife

Monday Morning Atheist

THE SWITCH SIX-STEP SERIES

The Switch Tool

WorkLife Caffeinated

WorkLife Thrive Guides

WorkLife Church Guide

ABOUT WORKLIFE.ORG

WorkLife's mission is to help working Christians Thrive at Work. People in every field of work can find hope, peace, and purpose in life's great mission field of work.

People benefit from:

- WorkLife's research and documented primary work issues that affect personal spiritual health at work.

- WorkLife's customized solutions that help individuals discover more purpose, balance, and peace at work.

- WorkLife's ability to partner with ministries, churches, and groups to equip and serve their members.

- WorkLife's curriculum, books, and innovative online coaching tools offered throughout the USA and internationally.

 Visit www.WorkLife.org.

MONDAY MORNING ATHEIST

Definition:
Someone who believes in God but who works like He does not exist.

When was the last time you thought about God at work?

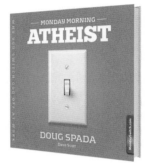

For millions of us, work doesn't seem to have a purpose other than a paycheck. Some feel that work is a kind of suffering that must be endured. How did work become such an empty, lifeless trade-off? There is a solution—it shows up in research, life stories, and in the Bible.

You will find it in this book. In Monday Morning Atheist, you will learn how to resist the lies that cause you to switch God OFF on the job.

Let's stop the switch!

Go To: www.WorkLife.org

THE SWITCH SIX-STEP SERIES
(Book+Study+DVD+Tools) All in One

Six Steps to God's Power on Mondays

The Journey begins! Interactive and personal—THE SWITCH Six-Step Series will simply and practically transform your Mondays. This interactive study leads you through an exhilarating journey of experiencing God's purpose, peace, and power in your work.

This multi-media, video-driven process includes:

*   The Monday Moan Meter
*   The Switch Quiz
*   THE SWITCH Book
*   Monday Text Alerts, and more.

It only requires 6 Mondays to SWITCH your entire work life. Designed for individual use, small group facilitation, or larger scale campaigns.

Whether you hate your job or love it, God has more for you than you imagine. His desire is for you to Thrive at work, not merely survive.

 Learn more at www.WorkLife.org.

THE SWITCH TOOL
WEEKLY ONLINE SUBSCRIPTION

How do you fight Monday Morning Atheism each week?

Interpersonal conflicts, job loss, ethical temptations, time crunches, and more.

The WorkLife Switch Tool is a self-directed, web-based system that helps people target and overcome the ever-changing issues that cause people to switch God off at work.

This tool acts as your work-week companion with powerful video clips, devotionals and quick-use tools that pack a powerful punch in a way that's easy to access. **GOAL: Staying Switched ON at work.**

Perfect for your busy lifestyle, plus creatively designed and delivered, The Switch Tool provides you with relevant teaching and help via a 2-part email/web format each week:

- Power ON tools for Mondays and
- Recharge toolbox on Thursdays.

 Visit www.WorkLife.org!

WORKLIFE CAFFEINATED

An Individual 30-week Growth Sequence

Wake Up! That's exactly what this tool will help you do—spiritually wake up. Each Caffeinated weekly segment is delivered to you via email & PDF and features:

- A situational mini story centered around a difficult work issue.
- A biblical teaching targeted to that unique work issue.
- Practical, real-life application with eternal perspective.

Reinforce your spiritual growth by taking the private mini assessment that scores how well you'd cope with that particular challenge at work. Whether it be a 1, or a 10, or somewhere in between, knowing your score can help you look for solutions and applications that will put you in a more prepared position at work. You can't help but grow in this structured discipleship process!

Go to www.WorkLife.org to get your work Caffeinated!

WORKLIFE THRIVE GUIDES

Biblically based studies to help you find Life in work: (for Individuals or Small Groups)

This comprehensive study series targets the 30 personal work issues that cause Monday Morning Atheism. Use these case studies each with biblical guidance in a group setting or for your own personal use.

Available individually, in bundles of five, or in a single bundle of all thirty modules.

Below is a sampling of Thrive Guide topics:

The Damage of a Hectic Pace, What God Thinks of Money, Co-workers and Sex, Fighting the Wrong Fight, Answering the Hard Questions, Eternal Balance Sheet, and many more...

▶ Visit WorkLife.org to learn more.

WORKLIFE CHURCH GUIDE

Mission Possible:
A Vision for Your Church
(For Church Leaders & Pastors)

Yes, it's possible to equip your people for missions right at the point of their greatest potential impact: their workplace! We've spent over a decade tackling the issue of how to empower and equip congregations for ministry in the workplace, and this guide gives you access to our research and first-hand experience.

This 80-page e-guide provides the following:

- An overview of why it's essential to address workplace ministry.
- A holistic biblical framework based on six principles for teaching and fostering a God-filled worklife.
- Implementation ideas, best practices, and next steps.

Not on staff at your church? Buy the e-guide for your pastor or elders so they can see the potential.

▶ **Visit** WorkLife.org **to learn more.**

you +

PASSING IT ON

Do you know someone suffering from Monday Morning Atheism?

Help people make The Switch at work by sharing
The Switch resources in your circle of influence.

+ virally communicate to your online networks
+ join a coworker and go through it together
+ start a weekly journey in your small group
+ share it throughout your network or business
+ inspire spiritual growth in your entire church

+ Go to *www.MondaySwitch.com* for more
ideas on sharing and to order resources!

Reach Your Church — Your Business — Your City

Join a select group of individuals who God is calling to champion The Switch Revolution! This is a global movement of working Christians committed to keeping God Switched ON Monday.

+ You might be the leader or possibly the catalyst that is used by God to inspire change in your entire group, church or business!

Simply take a small step and and find out now.

Investigate ways you can be a champion by visiting
▶ www.MondaySwitch.com.

MY PRAYERS & NOTES

MY PRAYERS & NOTES